Foundations of
Christian Ethics

D0862042

Paulist Press ◇ **New York** ◇ **Mahwah**

Library of Congress Cataloging-in-Publication Data
Dwyer, John C.
    Foundations of Christian ethics.

    1. Christian ethics—Catholic authors. I. Title.
BJ1294.D88   1987   241   87-13580
ISBN 0-8091-2908-6 (pbk.)

Published by Paulist Press
997 Macarthur Boulevard
Mahwah, N.J. 07430

Printed and bound in the United States of America

Contents

Foreword

Although this book is written by a Catholic, it uses the general term *Christian Ethics* in its title, because the New Testament is the hidden or overt basis of all the ethical reflection which it contains. As in other branches of theology, to the degree to which ethical reflection is based on the New Testament, it is deconfessionalized. And because the book maintains, among other things, that the specifically Christian element in ethics is not to be found in the realm of *content* but rather in that of motivation and empowerment, I hope that most of it will make sense to men and women who are not Christian, but who, whether they realize it or not, believe in God, in the sense that they admit the existence of values, not of their own making, which claim them totally and which have the right to make that claim.

The division between believers and unbelievers in our day is not between those who use the word "God" with confidence and those in whose vocabulary the word "God" does not appear. It is rather the division between those who hold to a moral relativism whose ultimate principle is "I must do whatever I *feel* is right for me," and those who recognize that there are objective values in life, which lay claim to us before we know it and whether or not we like it.

1

Moral relativism is profoundly inhuman, and under its aegis, the always fragile barrier between civilization and barbarism inevitably gives way. And yet in many ways, Christian moral reflection itself prepared the way for the apparent triumph of this relativism, because it spoke carelessly and inaccurately about the objective element in decision-making. Situation ethics (the attempt to give theological cover to moral relativism) is a destructive response to a real defect in traditional moral theory—that is, to the insistence that norms and standards of moral activity are *themselves* objective and not merely that they have a ground and basis in the objective order.

The Christian moral tradition has the resources to deal with relativism, but it can do this effectively only if it uses the greatest care in defining its terms. Furthermore, our defense of the objectivity of value will be successful only if we use terminology and methods of argument which can be understood by men and women today. For example, the *content* of the term "natural law" as used by Thomas Aquinas, is at the heart of all sound ethical reflection. But if we insist on using the term "natural law" itself in our discussions today, this will virtually guarantee misunderstanding.

Ethical reflection, and the decision to act on the conclusions derived from it, are really possible only for the *free* man or woman, but traditional moral theology had accepted an inadequate concept of freedom from pre-Christian Greek thought. It was a concept which made the defense of freedom very difficult, and it was instrumental in bringing about the over-emphasis on law which characterized much moral theology up to recent times. For this reason, this book proposes, in outline form, a biblical concept of freedom, and it finds precisely in this concept the uniquely Christian element in the morally good decision.

Perhaps more today than at any time in history, Catholics are asking about the role which they should assign to the teaching authority of their Church as they strive to make decisions about how to act rightly and well. They are asking about the nature of such authority and about the limits of dissent. This book outlines an approach to these problems which respects our twofold responsibility: our inalienable responsibility for making our own moral choices, and our acquired responsibility for, as Paul put it, "building up the Church." Because we are fortunate enough to live in an ecumenical age, I believe that these reflections will be of interest to Protestant Christians as well.

Finally, because all ethical theory, if it is not to degenerate into mere ideology, must issue in practical decisions about how to act, the final chapter offers a summary of the whole process of decision-making in a discussion on the nature of the Christian conscience and on the challenge of giving it the shape and form which it should have.

The views which are expressed in the following pages represent half a lifetime of reflection on what could be called the fundamental theology of ethical and moral commitment. Over many years I have learned much from many teachers, among whom two men deserve special mention: Paul Kennedy, S.J., of the Jesuit School of Philosophy and Theology at West Baden, Indiana; and Alfons Auer, of the Faculty of Catholic Theology of the University of Tübingen. Over the course of many years, I have read a series of position papers and lecture notes on a variety of moral questions, authored by a friend who has one of the most acute minds in the field of moral theology today—Rev. James O'Donohoe, of the Archdiocese of Boston. His work has influenced this book in many ways and I am indebted to him for many valuable insights. Over the past twenty years, I have learned much from my students, and many of them will have no difficulty in discerning their critical questions, in and behind many of the discussions in this book. For reasons too many and too deep to summarize in a few words, this book would never have been written, if it were not for my wife, Odile.

I am dedicating this book to Patrick Burns, S.J., a friend of many years. Many of the reflections and conclusions in this book emerged from discussions we have had at odd intervals over several decades, and even more of them have been inspired by his humanism and his humor which, in their depth and their coexistence, are so deeply Christian.

Moraga, California
December 1, 1986

1

Introduction

1.1 THE UNIQUE CHARACTER OF HUMAN EXISTENCE

The scope of this book is broader than the title might indicate; it is really about the *challenge* of being human, the challenge to become a person. It is important to emphasize this word *challenge,* because a truly human existence is not simply given to us, ready-made, and a truly human life does not come into being automatically. A truly human existence is an *achievement,* and it is one which is worthy of our best efforts. No more demanding, intriguing, fascinating task could be imagined. For each of us, a truly human existence is something not yet achieved, something for which we are searching. We are *summoned,* called to real existence and this is a call to advance beyond that partial achievement of personhood which characterizes our lives at any given moment. This call to become persons does not come to us from a mere object or from a "situation"; like every such call or summons, it comes not simply from a place but ultimately from a person.

What this means is that we cannot talk about the task of being human without raising the question of God. For the question of God is not really the question of whether there is a "supreme being" up there and out there, and it is certainly not the question of whether there is some kind of "cosmic consciousness" which is either indifferent to our concerns, or possibly even well-disposed toward them. The question of God is the question of whether human life makes sense; it is the question of whether our lives have a goal, a purpose. Quite simply, it is the question of whether there is a reason for our being here, or not. The questions which will be raised in the course of this book are really, though in disguised form, all reducible to one question: the question of God. It is in raising the moral question that we, and all human beings, encounter God.

Of course when we talk of "the challenge of becoming a person," this does not mean that we begin life as non-persons. But the phrase does point to the fact that, at any given moment, we are only partially in possession of our personhood and our identity, and that full personhood and identity always lie before us. The so-called "identity crisis" is not really an odd neurotic symptom, reserved to those with enough time and money to be able to afford such luxuries. It is an essential aspect of our human nature and it is part of the human condition.

Another way of appreciating the human challenge is to point out that a person is one who has a peculiar relationship to the future. The future is the "place" where we will have achieved real personhood, true identity, or will have lost it, and it is for this reason that a person is one who is essentially *open* to the future. The future is not simply the place where important things will happen to us; the real future is precisely that which we are constantly bringing about in our decisions *now*. The human mystery consists in the fact that the future (at least everything really important about the future) is in our own hands.

1.2 OUR DECISIONS AND OURSELVES

The task of becoming a person is one at which we will succeed or fail precisely in the choices or *decisions* which we make. There is nothing surprising about this, because it is in our decisions that we fashion our own future. To emphasize the importance of our choices and decisions in this way does not mean that our feelings and our sensations, our heredity and our environment are unimportant. They are all very important, but they *are* important because of what we *decide to do* about them, because of the *decisions* we make. Like most of the things in our lives, we have not chosen our heredity, and our environment is usually beyond our control. They are simply "there"—either imposed on us or simply "given" in our situation, and although they confront us with decisions of many kinds, we usually do not have the option of accepting or rejecting them. What we do have to decide is whether to let our*selves* be determined by these factors or to take responsibility and be *self-determining*, despite the constraints imposed by feeling, sensation, heredity, and environment.

These decisions which we make are not simply things that we *do*. We cannot distance ourselves from them, for they are a part of us, our very selves in action. Furthermore, although it is true that our decisions *reveal* who we are, they are more deeply a part of us than that would seem to imply. In our decisions *we create ourselves*. We are always underway toward our true selves, or away from them and it is through our decisions that we move along the right path or lose our way. There is one overwhelmingly important implication of this: our decisions are, at their deepest level, not merely decisions about how to *act;* they are decisions about *what to be* and about *who to be*.

1.3 FREEDOM

This aspect of our decision-making is at the very heart of our human mystery. Our being, our reality, who and what we really are, is something which we *decide* on. It is *we* who create ourselves, for we are not pre-programmed like the other animals. Rather, our specifically human task is to write our own program. This is not, of course, to deny that in the chemical and biological realms we are programmed by physical laws and genetic codes. But it is important to note that these "sub-programs" or subroutines do not determine our existence but simply provide the raw material which we are called on to organize and integrate into a truly human program. To put it simply, we are *free*.

We are free, not because we can act in an arbitrary way, and not because we can do "anything we please," no matter how stupid or destructive it is. If this were the case, freedom would hardly be a value. We are free because we can discover a call, a summons to be real persons, and because we have the power to respond to that call. We are free *because we have the power to create ourselves*. We are free because we can create valuable and authentic selves out of the *given* raw material (which is very often not of our own choosing). Paradoxically, we are free because we have the power to do as we *ought*.

1.31 Freedom and the Constraints and Limitations of Life

If freedom is defined simply as the absence of constraining or determining factors in our lives, then it is a simple task to prove that we are never free. From birth to death we are, at every moment, conditioned by a very large number of factors. We can often do little or nothing about their existence or their power to touch us, sometimes in very disturbing ways. However, freedom should *not* be defined as the absence of constraining factors in our lives. We are free because, although the more superficial levels of our existence are determined in ways over which we have little or no control, we can *refuse to remain* on the superficial level and we can refuse to let ourselves be defined by things. Our environment does determine a *part* of us; we are free because we can refuse to identify our persons, ourselves with that *part* of us.

We are more aware today, than at any time in history, of the many constraints which limit us, ranging from the popular cliché of "oppressive social structures" down to the various psychoses and neuroses which are germinally present even in the healthiest human psyche. However, these constraints do not *compete* with our free decisions, as though we could *either* affirm our freedom, *or* admit the existence of these constraining factors in our lives. The real question is not "either/or" but rather a quite different one: "What will we *do* about these constraints?" The very factors in life over which we have little or no control are the raw material out of which we are called to create ourselves. Freedom is not the absence of limiting and constraining factors in our lives; freedom is the ability and the power to make use of them. We are not called to create persons in the abstract but in the concrete.

Sometimes moral theologians or writers in the field of ethics speak about factors which *limit* freedom—among them, fear, ignorance, immaturity, social conditioning, and many others. They do this to show that, under certain circumstances, we may be less than fully responsible for our actions. However, it would be better to see in these factors not limitations of freedom, but rather a limiting or narrowing of the area in which we are called to work out our freedom. Fear, for example, may simply prevent certain options from being real possibilities, but we are still called to fashion a real self, and the best one possible, out of the limited possibilities which remain.

In this book we will look at the mystery of freedom from many different vantage points, but we can begin by pointing out that, for one very obvious reason, the fact that we are free cannot be reasonably or intelligently denied. Those who deny freedom spend much time and effort trying to get us to accept their views. They seem to feel that, on seeing the evidence, we will be convinced of the truth of their position, and we will accept it. But *to be able to see the truth and then to opt for it when seen is to be free.* The vocal denial of freedom is as incoherent and self-contradictory as the vocal denial of truth.

1.4 GOOD AND BAD, RIGHT AND WRONG

We have the power to respond to a call, but we can also fail to respond. We can succeed in becoming persons, but we can also fail. Since success in the task of becoming a person is something which we intuitively call "good," it seems appropriate to call those decisions "good" or "right" in which we create the selves we are called to be, and to call those in which we fail at this task "bad" or "wrong." We will, of course, have to ask *why* it seems appropriate to speak this way, and what the words "good" and "bad" mean when they are used this way; and this means that we will be asking *ethical* questions. Ethics is the science of human conduct, and it issues from critical reflection on the meaning of the words "good" and "bad" as applied to human activity, and especially to decision-making. The basic ethical question is simply, "What does it mean to act rightly and well?" This question implies many others: Is a choice right simply because it is the choice of something which I want to do? Are there ways of acting which are worthy of being chosen and others which are not, independently of whether I know this and like it? That is, is this "worthiness," this quality which is responsible for the fact that I *should* act in a certain way, a quality which is *there* whether I know it, admit it, like it, or not?

These questions can be phrased in terms of some practical problems, and this will bring them from the seemingly abstract to the obviously concrete. Is lying (the act of deliberately making statements which are not true) acceptable if it helps me make a good profit in selling some product which no one would buy if I ever told the truth about it? Or is it justifiable if it helps me avoid blame for some mistake I made? Is it desirable human conduct to terminate my marriage if I find a more "fulfilling" or "enriching" relationship with another? Is abortion acceptable if it solves the problem of the unwanted pregnancy? Or perhaps if it solves the problem of the truly tragic pregnancy?

These questions are simple enough, but finding answers which are sound and convincing is anything but simple. It is not easy to discover ways of acting which in and of themselves are worthy of being chosen, and in matters of importance it is always difficult. But the serious and persevering effort to find this elusive value (that is, the way of acting which is worthy of our choice) is the pursuit which, above all others, gives meaning to our lives.

The most important contribution of Christian thought to ethical reflection down through the years has been the conviction that we can fulfill the task of being human only if there *are* ways of acting (which we can describe with some clarity) which in and of themselves

are worthy of being chosen, and others which are unworthy of being chosen, whether we know it, admit it,
and like it, or not. This position is closely connected with
the traditional Christian conviction that God has made
us and our world for a purpose; it is closely connected
with the conviction that there are ways of acting which
promote and respect that purpose and others which
impede and frustrate the attainment of that purpose.
And, finally, this position is closely connected with the
conviction that we can discover and respect these purposes, and that our task is to do just that. At the center
of the Christian tradition is the conviction that those who
reject the objectivity of value are engaging in the only
fundamental and radical evil of which we human beings
are capable, even though this rejection is defended today
by many who should know better, and is propagated almost universally, in simplified form, by the media. But
it is very important to see precisely what the fundamental
evil here consists in: *not* the wrong which people are
doing today, and which is not much different from the
wrong they have been doing since the beginning of re-
corded history. It consists rather in the widespread tendency today to insist that each of us is a law unto him/
herself and that there is no one and nothing outside of
us in terms of which our actions and choices are to be
judged.

Note carefully that traditional Christian thought does
not necessarily assert that there are certain actions "out
there" which are "good in themselves" and others which
are "bad in themselves," or sinful. For clarity and accuracy, it is better, when we are talking about ethical
choices, to reserve the words "good" and "right," as well
as "bad" and "wrong," for our *decisions,* and not to use

them in speaking of actions without reference to the decisions which bring them about.

1.41 Faith, Reason, and the Moral Choice

In the rest of this chapter, we will survey some of the questions and problems which will appear in the course of the book, and by way of introduction we will state briefly the direction in which the answers will take us. But before we do, there is one final point which belongs in these preliminary comments on good and evil, right and wrong. Our reflection on all of these questions may proceed solely on the basis of *reason* (here the word means "an intelligent examination of human experience"), and in this case we speak of *philosophical ethics.* On the other hand, our reflection may make use of revelation (specifically the Old and New Testaments), and in this case we speak of *theological ethics* (the term used mostly by Protestants) or *moral theology* (the usual Catholic term). As we will see, this distinction between philosophical and theological ethics, although traditional, is far too neat, and really does not do justice to the role of faith in the moral life of the Christian.

1.5 NORMS AND STANDARDS

To speak of ways of acting which, in themselves, are worthy of being chosen, even before we know it and even without our recognizing it, raises a good question: "Why is it that some actions are worthy or unworthy of being chosen, and what is it which gives them that quality and which accounts for that characteristic?" This question is often called the question of an *objective norm or standard of morality.*

As we have seen, many people today reject any moral norms or standards which would be based on the existence of values outside of us and they argue that the only valid norms are purely internal: "be true to yourself," "do what you feel is right," "follow your conscience." But at best these so-called internal norms beg the question. To which self am I to be true? Not only do we change, but we ourselves are divided, vacillating in respect to almost every important decision; within each of us there are competing selves clamoring for attention, and it is possible that the self which I am at the moment is not the self which I ought to be. It is also possible that "what I *feel* is right" might actually not *be* right at all. It is even possible that my conscience, in a given case, might be the product of self-deception, or might be a hypocritical facade for selfishness. As we will see, these internal norms, such as conscience, make sense only if they are based on something *outside* of us as individuals, which can rightfully lay total claim to us.

Many Christians are aware of this fact, and they argue that it is God's law which determines which ways of acting are worthy of being chosen and which are unworthy. Those who hold this view usually think of the Ten Commandments as God's law in the Old Testament; to these they add the moral imperatives taught by Jesus (which they have sometimes called the "law of Christ") and, for Catholics, the laws of the church, and for Protestants, the moral traditions of their respective churches. However, as we have seen, a good understanding of the New Testament shows that, although Jesus made uncompromising demands on his followers, his words are misunderstood if they are interpreted as law. And it has become clear that in Paul's statement, in Romans 10:4, that "Christ is the end of the law," he was not referring simply to the Jewish law, but to *all* ways of saving oneself by obedience to religious law, which would then give one some kind of hold or claim on God. It is a great distortion of Christian existence to see it essentially as a life lived in obedience to law.

Furthermore, if freedom is the power to create the self, the power to respond to a call, it must consist in more than following orders or submitting to a higher authority. When some modern atheists criticize the "god" who would keep human beings in this kind of tutelage, they are perfectly correct. The real God creates free men and women, not serfs, and he intends that we create our true selves by opting for courses of action which our intelligence shows us to be worthy of our choice.

1.51 Natural Law

Christian tradition has often suggested that it is in *nature* itself or in *natural law* that we find the norms and standards which we need if we are to measure proposed ways of acting, and to determine whether or not they are worthy of being chosen. But both of these terms are easily misunderstood. Today we think of "nature" as referring to the natural world which confronts us, and we may think particularly of the beauty or of the power or of the mysteries of nature; and we think of "law" as being simply "a piece of legislation." But the phrase "natural law" means something quite different: it means "the purposes and goals which are inherent in things because God made them" or "the natural goals which are simply part of the reality of things." There are three implications which are part of traditional thinking about the natural law. The first is that things and persons *have* a finality and a purposiveness which is part of their very existence. The second is that an intelligent examination of ourselves and of the things of our world will reveal what this finality and purposiveness is. The third implication is that the finality, the purposiveness of things, is what we must respect when we make decisions about them, and therefore it is that which is *normative* in our decision-making.

The concept of natural law *in this sense* is indispensable for clear thinking in moral matters, but there is one serious problem with the way it was used. It was often implied that God fixed the purposes of things at the moment of creation and decreed that they remain the same forever. But God's creation is not static and immobile. God created (or, even better, *is creating*) the world and has given it the power to change and evolve. In the course of this evolutionary process, new goals and purposes emerge which replace those of earlier times, and they merit and demand our respect. The approach of Thomas Aquinas (the thirteenth century theologian who has had such a profound influence on Christian thought) is a very good one here. Thomas did not think of natural law as the sum total of all of the purposes of everything in the world, fixed forever by God at the moment of creation. For Thomas, natural law is primarily *human intelligence* itself, as it strives to grasp the complexities of a situation, and as it strives to discern all of the purposes which are proper to the persons and things which are part of that situation.

1.52 Different Meanings of the Term "Norm of Morality"

Even from this brief introduction, it seems clear that when people speak of norms or standards of morality, they are actually referring to a number of different things, three of which should be mentioned here. *First,* they may be referring to a clear and detailed list of "do's" and "don'ts"—a list which is not of our own making, but which simply confronts each of us. In such a case, the only moral task would be to determine whether or not a given line of conduct falls under one of the commandments or prohibitions. *Second,* they may be referring to a *description* of those ways of acting which are worthy of being chosen and of others which are unworthy. *Third,* they may be referring to a *set of instructions* about how to fashion such a description.

The first of these meanings mechanizes human conduct in a way which is unworthy of the human person and virtually rejects the role of intelligence in decision-making. The other two meanings of the phrase "norms or standards of morality" are both legitimate, but they should not be confused. The third should be called *practical advice about fashioning norms.* The second, and it alone, should be called *a norm or standard of morality* in the proper sense.

But are norms in this sense *objective?* Do they exist independently of us? Or—and this is a better question—do they have a basis outside of us? Many today who are concerned (as they should be) about the contemporary tendency to "do one's own thing," and to do stupid, destructive, and appalling things which they "feel are right," want to argue that the norms and standards of morality are objective, in the sense that they are "out there," independent of us and preexisting us. However, although their intentions are laudable, those who speak this way are not speaking accurately. Norms are always *judgments which we make,* and the great moral task is not to conform to ready-made norms but to create good ones for ourselves. Norms themselves are not objective in the sense of being "out there." Ways of acting or patterns of activity are "there"—ways which are creative or destructive, human or inhuman. It is these ways or patterns of activity which provide the *objective basis* for moral norms, but the norms themselves are deliberately intelligent judgments, which are made about ways of acting which are really and objectively human or inhuman. What is "out there" is a real world, the meaning and purpose of which can be either understood and respected, or ignored and despised. It is our task to use our intelligence to discern the finality and purposiveness of this world and of everything in it.

1.6 THE FUNDAMENTAL MORAL IMPERATIVE

This leads to an interesting conclusion: the fundamental moral imperative is not "to do what we feel is right," nor is it to respect an arbitrary set of commands and prohibitions. The fundamental moral imperative is to do all that is in our power to insure that "what we feel is right" is the result of a *sound judgment,* based on *the way things really are,* and on the ends and purposes which are inherent in things even before we come on the scene.

This leads to an interesting question: Is there any way of acting which is so essentially and inherently human that we cannot reject it without being responsible for that rejection, and without turning our backs on our very selves? Are there any kinds of acts which are so totally a denial of our humanity that the excuse "I did not know" or "I was ordered to do it" will never be acceptable?

There is a good answer to this question: unlike the other animals, who are simply in the world and a part of it, we are called to be *aware of the world, to understand it, to be intrigued by it, and to love it.* Our most fundamental human task is to be attentive, open to reality, so that we may think correctly about it, respect it, and act responsibly toward it. This task is so fundamental that to deny it, to deliberately remain in the dark, is to reject our human responsibility and to refuse to be human—and this is the only real evil of which we are capable. This means that the one absolutely certain moral imperative for us is this: "Do all that is reasonably in your power to make deliberately intelligent judgments about the world, about other people, and about your own self, so that you may understand the meaning of each and discover the ways of acting which help each attain its meaning and fulfill its purpose." Although, at first sight, this principle seems very general, if we accept it, it will guide our thought and action even in matters of detail.

This has an important consequence which we will examine later: making morally good decisions consists essentially in developing techniques of finding the truth, of being attentive to the real world and its demands, and of discovering the real issues which are at stake. In fact, the enduring commitment to develop such techniques is at the heart of the morally good human existence. This shows that the really important moral decisions are often made, not when we are under pressure, but *when we prepare for those times when we are going to be under pressure,* and deliberately take time to anticipate problems, fashion sound policy, and hold to worthy ideals.

1.61 The Role of Intelligence in the Moral Life

What has just been said implies that intelligence itself, and respect for intelligent ways of acting, play a preponderant role in making morally good decisions. This, of course, does not mean that having a high IQ or a "good education" (in the usual sense) is the key to good moral living. Nor does it mean that the clever will inherit not only the earth but heaven as well. Intelligence should not be confused either with reasoning, or with the perception of relationships, or with the ability to find means which are suited to attain a given end, or with general cleverness. Reasoning is the ability to draw valid conclusions from premises which are given—something which is quite useful, but which is only a part of intelligence and not really the heart of the matter at all. The perception of relationships is something which can be programmed into a computer with only moderate difficulty (if we are not too fussy about the word "perception"). And the ability to find means suited to attain a given end is an application of *controlling* reason—a subordinate function of intelligence, but not to be identified with it. And we often think of the clever person as one who uses controlling reason to "get ahead in life," without raising questions about the validity of the goal or the moral quality of the means.

Real intelligence is something quite different. Properly understood, intelligence is *the act of being consciously present to the real world, aware of who we and others really are, aware of what is real.* It is the power and the act of being open to the real, of understanding it, and of acting respectfully toward it. Real intelligence has strong emotional components, because emotion, when properly understood, is the experience of the attractiveness of the real (or of the repulsiveness of the pseudo-real). True intelligence is rooted in respect for the real, and its ultimate root is faith in God.

To act intelligently means simply to strive to understand things as they *really* are. This concern for reality is important, because it underlines the fact that if we are going to act rightly and well, it is not enough to "do what we feel is right"; we have to make decisions which *really are right* because they are based on our commitment to discover *the way things really are.*

1.62 Coping with Disagreement

But it is precisely in our search to discover the truth, the way things really are, that difficulties occur. Our important decisions rarely involve a clear-cut choice between being creative and human on the one hand, and being destructive and inhuman on the other. The problem in life is that one and the same decision is often creative from one point of view and destructive from another. Often enough, in real life, human values seem to be in conflict, and it is especially here that good techniques have to be developed for discovering the values at stake. The classic approach of moral theology here is interesting and worthy of examination. It started with the assumption that practically all problem cases arose because one of our actions would simultaneously have two effects—one good and one bad—and then it developed techniques to determine whether or not it was permissible to perform such an action. The principle was called, not unreasonably, the *principle of the double effect*. What the principle of the double effect affirmed was that the "bad" effect could not be intended as an end or a means, and that the good effect should be so significant, so important, that it justified tolerating the bad effect.

When carefully applied, the principle of the double effect was a rather good tool for analyzing issues and motives, but there were some problems with it which suggest that another, simpler approach might be better. Those who formulated the principle usually spoke as though actions and effects could be called "good" or "bad" (in the moral sense). But, as we have seen, these words are used accurately in speaking only of our *decisions*, and not of the actions which follow upon them.

In problem cases, we have to be aware of the fact that the destruction of human value can never be intended. The real question is that of determining the *relative importance* of the values to be gained or lost. And this means doing all in our power to make correct value judgments, by being open to the evidence, and drawing the right conclusions from it, so that we may respond appropriately. This implies that we should make a deliberate attempt to eliminate factors which interfere with clear thinking. It involves conferring with others who have expertise in the area, and it means utilizing all the resources which the wisdom of the past puts at our disposal. It involves (as the exercise of intelligence always does) discipline, asceticism, and humility. Starting from the basic principle that our task is to discover the objective values which are present everywhere in life, our task will be that of fashioning practical norms in all areas of life by utilizing all of the means just enumerated. The last question to be asked before making the decision is always this: "Have I done all that is *reasonably* in my power to discover what the real values are and to weigh them properly?"

1.7 THE ROLE OF FAITH

Faith is a much misunderstood word. It is not a substitute for understanding and it is not an irrational or unmotivated leap in the dark. Rightly understood, faith is a supremely intelligent act, because it is the act of knowing God as he wants to be known, and as he really is. And this is the basis of real knowledge of the world, of others, and of ourselves. (God may be known under his own name, or he may be known under "pseudonyms"—even by agnostics or atheists; and if he is, then real faith, admittedly in an incomplete form, may be found outside Christianity and even among those who profess not to believe in God.)

But this definition of faith leads to a good question: Is there anything different about the decisions which Christians make (at least if they make them *as Christians*)? Naturally, Christians have always asserted that there is, but there is much disagreement on what constitutes the specifically Christian element. Some have argued that there are additional obligations which are binding on Christians, and that they are found in the Old Testament and the New— for example, the Ten Commandments and the teachings of Jesus. However others, more correctly, have pointed out that it is better to look for the specifically Christian element not in the realm of *content* but rather in something about the *way*, the *manner* in which, the *conditions* under which the decision is made. According to this view, Christians know (or at least *should* know) something which others do not, and this knowledge *liberates* them in such a way that they are able to make good decisions.

But is such liberation really needed? It is, and for a strange reason. Although we are made for the truth and deeply desire objective value, at least at times we refuse to search for the truth and we refuse to recognize objective values. Instead of thinking correctly so that we can choose rightly, we choose wrongly and try to make our thinking conform to our morally bad choices. We rationalize, trying to convince ourselves that we are doing nothing wrong, even though we know that we are.

There is something exceedingly strange at work in this paradox, this tension, this contradiction. Within us, there is a discrepancy between what we are and what we should be, which seems to contradict our very nature. There is something wrong, "out of order," at the very center of the human personality. It is not simply that our intelligence is limited or that we are slow to discover the truth; it is rather that we turn away from the truth. Paul put it simply in the seventh chapter of his letter to the Romans: "The good which I would like to do, I do not do; what I do is the evil which I hate." It is here that we face the problem of evil, and of human sinfulness, in all of its simplicity and all of its depth.

It is clear that no one chooses evil *as* evil, and that no one chooses a non-value as such. No one chooses to destroy value *simply and solely* for the sake of destroying value. Non-values and destructiveness must first be masked as values before we can choose them, but *it is precisely in this most fundamental of choices*—the choice to let falsehood and destruction wear the mask of truth and creativity—that real evil lies.

Our tendency to act in this way is at the very heart of what the Christian tradition has called "original sin"—not a personal act, but something very much like a force or power which moves us to reject God and the truth of God and to substitute a lie of our own making. In yielding to this tendency, we become personally guilty, because, although we know that we are made for the truth, we deliberately suppress it (and a sign of our deliberation is that we try to suppress our awareness of what we are doing, even from ourselves). Paul speaks of this situation with great power in Romans 1:18–31. He traces all human pride, deception, and unpitying hatred to the fact that "Although men knew God, they did not treat him as God, and did not give thanks to him, but they made fools of themselves so that their senseless hearts were darkened. They thought that they were wise, but they were fools . . . and they exchanged the truth of God for falsehood." Original sin is an inborn tendency, within all of us, but it is a tendency which we ratify, and in ratifying it, we sin.

To speak of original sin is not, of course, to argue

for the historicity of the myth of creation and of the story of the fall of Adam and Eve; it is simply to take seriously this destructive tendency in human nature. The careful and honest observation of human nature leads to the conclusion that there is something flawed, something wrong, with human beings as they are, and that the human animal must be overhauled before we can create the selves we are called to be, and before we can discover the truth and do it. This basic re-creation of the human being is the offer and the claim of the Christian message. In Mark's Gospel, it is the "good news" of Mark 1:14, which is defined in 2:17 as sharing in the unconditional acceptance of God. In Paul it is the "good news which works for the salvation (healing!) of all" in Romans 1:16. In John 8:38, it is the "truth (which) will make you free."

The human tragedy is that we our*selves* are divided. But according to both the Gospels and Paul's writings, faith functions by healing the divided self. The New Testament is the offer of faith, because it is the story of an enormous gift which is given, and it is the story of the transforming effects of that gift on human life. There is no doubt that the New Testament makes demands on us and claims us, but it does not do this as law. The New Testament claims us because it is the story of God's gift of himself to us in Jesus Christ. Unlike all other gifts, the gift of self, which another makes to me, forces me to raise a very special kind of question. It forces me to ask *what I am saying about myself if I accept the gift*—what I am saying about the kind of person I am and the kind of person I want to be. It forces me to admit that I need this gift if I am to become a whole person. This means that to accept this gift is to accept the totally new kind of person I can become as a result of this gift. To the degree that I have become such a new person and am aware of it, certain ways of acting become inevitable, and other ways of acting become inconceivable. This is the case, not because a new law is being imposed from the outside, but rather because certain kinds of activity have become impossible for the new self that I now am as a result of God's gift. The New Testament is the story both of a gift and of a demand, but the only demand is to accept the gift—fully, totally, unrestrictedly.

1.8 CONSCIENCE

We have spoken often about ways of acting which, in and of themselves, are worthy of being chosen, and about others which are not. But obviously, people do not agree on these matters, and they make different judgments on the way they ought to act. Presumably they cannot all be right, but are they responsible for being wrong? This raises the question of conscience, and the question of the obligation of following one's own conscience and of respecting the conscience of others.

Conscience is popularly understood as the "still, small voice within" which tells us whether we have done right or wrong—or, perhaps more importantly, tells us whether a projected decision will be morally good or bad. This notion of conscience is not bad, but neither is it accurate enough to help us to distinguish conscience from some other things which it emphatically *is not*—for instance, taboo, the super-ego, the weight of mere customs and conventions.

Conscience could be defined as the *judgment* that I make about a concrete decision which I am contemplating. It is the judgment that asserts that I *should* decide the question in one way rather than another. But when the word is used in this sense, it would be better to use the term "conscience judgment." We could then use the word "conscience" to refer to the ability to make such judgments habitually, and a "good" conscience would consist in the habitual practice of making such judgments on the basis of the commitment to discover the truth about God, about the world, and about ourselves. This ability consists in the habitual presence of a number of other, deeper judgments about the reality of values which are independent of us, about the essential values of life, and the general normative judgments which we make in the different areas of life—social and economic justice, honesty and integrity, professional responsibility, a human approach to sexuality.

We will talk later in this book about some distinctions which have to be made in discussing conscience, but here we have to raise a good (and typically modern) question: "Do we have an obligation to follow our consciences?" The answer is that we do have such an obligation *but only when we have used all reasonable means to locate the real values in life.* This means that, rather than speaking of the obligation to *follow* one's conscience, it is far more accurate to speak of the obligation of *forming* one's conscience in the right way, by committing ourselves willingly and deliberately to the truth. To form one's conscience in the right way is to be deliberately discerning, and to intend to distinguish real value from pseudo-value, common sense from common nonsense. We form our consciences correctly by developing clever plans for promoting and protecting the real values in life, for foreseeing difficulties which may arise, and for preventing them. To form one's conscience well is to be willing to learn from others, to observe the way intelligent and responsible people have acted in the past and are acting now. To form one's conscience is to do what is in one's power to remove ignorance of the facts and of the principles involved in a given case. In summary, we form our consciences well when we are critical, when we call into question the judgments we have made, and when we ask whether they have been made on the basis of evidence or on the basis of slogans, whether they result from a commitment to the truth or from an elaborate attempt to delude ourselves. To make the essential point again: *our task as human beings is not to follow our consciences but to form them.* It is here that the Gospel, the Christian message, plays its central role in our moral lives.

The Christian message about God who accepts us unconditionally brings us the most profound liberation possible. It solves the problem of our insecurity (which is at the root of all of the moral evil we do) by offering us total security as a pure gift. If God accepts us, then there are no "terminal" threats, which would have the power to destroy us for good. God's acceptance frees us from the pseudo-values of life, and it frees us from using our intelligence manipulatively to pay homage to these pseudo-values. God's acceptance frees us to use our intelligence to *be there* for the neighbor.

Genuine faith makes the good conscience judgment possible. The good conscience judgment and the good moral act (they are really one and the same) are completely human, fully intelligent, and free acts. As is always the case, faith does not conflict with human intelligence and freedom; rather, it empowers them, makes them possible. This is the essential point if we are to understand the relation of faith to the morally good decision.

The task of moral theology is not to discover a set of preexistent norms and then to order us to submit to them. The task of moral theology is to lead us to see that we will fulfill the task of becoming persons in the full sense of the word by fashioning sound norms of action, which are based on the understanding of the real world which God has created—a world which is also our world because he gave it to us. The act of forming the Christian conscience is essentially the fashioning of such norms.

1.9 WHAT WE WILL TRY TO DO

The purpose of this book is to develop a good method of raising the right questions about what it means to act in a morally good way, and to develop a method of finding good answers to these questions. The approach relies very strongly on the New Testament, because it is my conviction that this document offers a definitive solution to the problems of living and dying in a truly human way. But the techniques developed, and the answers proposed (and there are such answers, because it is impossible to develop methods of doing anything, without at the same time giving some examples), are those which I hope we can share with our non-Christian or post-Christian relatives and friends, simply because they are valid in *human* terms.

My purpose here is not to present my personal solution to a number of specific moral problems, but rather to outline a method or manner of approaching such problems which is demonstrably Christian and which works. However, neither is it my purpose (even though my approach owes much to the Catholic tradition) to summarize what is sometimes called "the Church's position" or "the teaching of the Church." The reasons for this should be obvious by now: in many cases there are significant differences in teaching in the Catholic Church; and, above all, when we talk about "the Church's position," we have to realize that those who have special teaching authority *in* the Church are not to be *identified* with the Church. However, precisely for this reason, it is important for Catholics to know how to make use of teaching authority in the Church, and of what has been taught, in order to make good moral choices, and there is a section near the end of the book which deals with this question—a section which will, I believe, be of interest to Protestant Christians for a variety of reasons, foremost among them the fact that Christians can no longer afford a theology which is not ecumenical in its concerns and in its intent.

In this chapter we have said just a few words about most of the questions of Christian ethics and moral theology. In the following chapters we will go more deeply into each of these questions, and strive to outline a method, a technique, and an approach for coping with moral questions which will be authentically Christian, and which is *therefore* intelligent, idealistic, and realistic.

2

Good and Evil,
Right and Wrong

2.1 THE BASIC QUESTIONS

What does it mean to act rightly and well? What is a "good" life as distinct from a "bad" one? We tend to answer questions like these intuitively, on the basis of hunches or feelings, and there is much disagreement, both in theory and in practice. But these questions are too important to allow the answers to be dictated by our vague feelings or our spontaneous hunches. We are called upon, because we are human, to *think* our way through questions and problems like these, and to find solutions which make sense.

There is an interesting way of doing this. We will examine a very popular contemporary approach to decision-making, which is known as "situation ethics," and which is often proposed as the only ethical system that is worthy of truly modern men and women. If we can show that the answers which situation ethics offers to the basic ethical questions are worse than useless, we will be well underway toward solving a number of fundamental ethical problems.

2.2 SITUATION ETHICS

To the question "What must I do to act rightly and well?" there is one answer which we hear more often than any other in our day: "I must always do what I feel is right for me. I must not impose my views of right and wrong on you, and (*above all!*) you must not impose your views on me. For after all, who is to say who is right?" This view is defended theoretically under the heading of "situation ethics," and there it is often given a theological cover: "There are no objective standards for human activity; I must always act in what I perceive to be a loving way, by letting the situation, in all of its uniqueness, speak to me." Behind the rhetoric about love there seems to lurk the suspicion that general norms or standards of action are abstract, and cannot really do justice to the unique character of each situation.

But far more dangerous than this "theological rhetoric" is the fact that this same view is proposed on virtually all levels of society as the only one appropriate for a truly modern person. It is omnipresent in popular literature and in the media. It is widely taught on all levels of public education; it is the bottom line in virtually all "values clarification" courses, and it is often portrayed as the only alternative to accepting the views of the "Moral Majority" in their entirety. In the past two decades it has made significant inroads among Christians, and for various reasons, many teachers, as well as ministers and priests, found that they were not able to give a convincing refutation of situation ethics in either its popular or its more theoretical form.

This view ("I must do what I feel is right for me . . . ") seems to be accepted without comment and without criticism by the overwhelming majority of our contemporaries.

And it is precisely this fact which constitutes the most serious ethical problem of the day, because the acceptance of "what I feel is right" as the ultimate moral standard may well be the only true degeneracy of which the human being is capable, now or at any time in history.

2.21 The Ambiguity of "Doing What I Feel Is Right for Me"

The phrase "I must do what I feel is right for me" can mean a number of different things, although two meanings seem most common. The first emphasizes the words "I" and "me" and underlines the uniqueness and individuality of the decision, and the "freedom" with which it is made. ("Freedom" is defined by those who hold this position as "the absence of coercion.") The implication is that if I am not coerced in making a decision, then it will be "the right one for me." In other words, the source of the rightness of the decision is precisely the fact that I am "free" in making it, in the sense that no one else has forced his ideas or values on me. The second interpretation of "doing what I feel is right for me" tacitly recognizes certain difficulties in the first, and argues that the phrase really means "being true to my real, genuine, authentic self in all of the decisions which I make." Both of these interpretations deserve examination.

If the goodness and rightness of a decision rest solely on the fact that I am not coerced and do not accept any scale of values other than my own—that is, that I am "free" in the deficient sense of freedom which we have mentioned above—then no one could ever call any of my decisions "bad" or "wrong," assuming that I was acting in the way I wanted to. This interpretation could be called "the Auschwitz principle of morality," since it provides a clear and logical justification for Auschwitz and for all other forms of inhumanity which human beings have ever perpetrated on each other in the course of history. For, after all, what gives me the right to dictate my code of morality to the man at the door of the gas ovens, pushing victims in by the thousands—or perhaps more appropriately, what gives me the right to dictate my code of morality to his superiors? Many, and probably most, in this appalling chain of command were "doing what they felt was right for them."

Although logical enough, this principle does seem to lead to some undesirable conclusions: even defenders of situation ethics feel the need to say something negative about Auschwitz; and therefore most of them prefer the second interpretation given above of "doing what I feel is right for me"; they tell us that what they really mean by the principle is this: "I must be true to my real self." This is often expressed in the form: "What is right for me is not necessarily right for you"—a particularly sloppy form of relativism which really denies that there are any standards by which the conduct of the individual ought to be measured. The problem is that unless there are such standards, terms like "authentic self" are devoid of meaning.

The real question, of course, is this: How do I know what is real and authentic in myself? The assumption behind "doing what I feel is right for me" in the sense of "being true to my authentic self" is that some of my desires proceed from deeper, more "real" levels of the self, while others come from more superficial, less "real" levels of the self. But how am I to tell them apart? Which "I" is the real one? Is the self which I am now more real than the one whose values I accepted last year? Does the passage of time guarantee growth in authenticity and genuinity? If *I* decide at any given moment which self is genuine and if I decide that the values of the moment are the really significant ones, then I have reverted to the Auschwitz principle, and out of respect for the principle of "doing what I feel is right," I will never be able to say a reproving word as the innocent are loaded into the gas ovens by the thousands. And, of course, with *both* of these interpretations of "doing what I feel is right," the most serious problem remains: What is it which makes this decision "right" for me? My *feeling*? If so, then the Auschwitz principle wins again.

2.22 " . . . Provided I Do Not Hurt or Harm Anyone Else"

In the face of these problems, defenders of the principle of "doing what I feel is right" usually assure us that what they really meant was "doing what I feel is right for me, provided that I don't hurt or harm anyone else." This proviso seems, at first sight, to solve some of the problems mentioned above, but it also raises some interesting questions.

The very fact that I must impose the second condition implies that there must be some decisions (or perhaps many, or most) which I *feel* are right for me but which, in point of fact, *are not right, not good at all.* And this implies something of even greater importance: there are decisions which are good and right (and others which are bad and wrong) *regardless of what I feel is right for me.* If this is true, then we have made real progress, because if ways of acting which result in hurting or harming others are unworthy of being chosen *regardless of how we feel,* then at least it will be possible to address problems like Auschwitz.

However, even with this new principle of "doing what we feel is right, provided we do not hurt another," some serious questions remain unanswered. In fact, even if we state this new principle in the most positive way—"It is a good thing to make decisions which respect others and which show care not to hurt or harm them"—the question which immediately comes to mind is this: "Who decides what ways of acting are hurtful or harmful to others?" Is "hurting" or "harming" another simply what I *decide* hurts them or harms them? If so, then we are back on square one. I may, for example, decide that it is a good thing to burn heretics at the stake, because the threat of such a frightful death is the only thing which will make them return to the true faith (and the threat, if carried out, will be of the greatest help to others, because it will prevent them from suffering the most serious harm possible—the loss of the true faith). Hopefully, not all will accept this reasoning, and therefore there will be disagreement on the question of which decisions are hurtful or harmful to others. But in the case of such disagreement, whose judgment is to prevail? That of the stronger party, or of the one able to force acceptance of his/her decision? If so, then we have reverted to the Auschwitz principle.

2.23 The Consensus of Society

Note carefully that the principle itself—we should decide in such a way that we respect others and take care not to hurt them—is not by any means a bad or useless principle. On the contrary, it can be a very good one, but *only if some way can be found to identify such decisions and to settle disagreements about them.* An approach which is very common today is to find such a norm in a *democratically reached consensus* or in the *consensus of society.* According to this approach, those decisions are hurtful or harmful which, when judged by the accepted standards of society, result in harm to others. But three interesting questions surface immediately.

First, which society's standards must I accept? No nation today is homogeneous, and we all live at one and the same time in many societies. Are the standards of my family, my peer group (or that of my parents), my tribe, my city, my ethnic group, my country, the *right* ones? Or perhaps the standards of those who share the same social and economic background as I do? Suppose that practically everyone in one or another of these groups, or even the overwhelming majority of all those people, about whose standards I know anything at all, decide that slavery is acceptable, because it does not infringe upon the inalienable rights of human beings (perhaps because those enslaved are "not really human beings at all"). Or suppose that an overwhelming majority decide that war is an acceptable instrument of national policy, or, more specifically, that all young men should register for the draft, and that those who refuse should be severely punished. Or suppose that there is almost universal agreement that capital punishment is an acceptable solution to the crime problem. *Do I then act wrongly if I refuse to accept these decisions of society, or if I reject the consensus of the dominant social group?*

But there is another side to this first question. There is a great deal of variability in contemporary standards. Some people today argue that individual life has no real value and that only the collective counts (although this sounds suspiciously like suggesting that a very large number of zeros will add up to one). Others assert that human beings exist to extract the maximum amount of pleasure from life, while still others feel that it is our task to be well-adjusted, or to conform to the group's expectations for us. (But can we avoid asking what gives the group the *right* to have these expectations for us?) Still others affirm that the only valid standard is one's own self-image and that one must be "true to him/herself"—perhaps an "outgoing" or "involved" or a "fun" person, or perhaps even a "conscientious" person. But which of these self-images is valid, genuine, authentic?

And a second question is equally serious: Are we to accept the standards of contemporary society, or those of societies of earlier times? And if we choose contemporary standards, do we do this because these standards are *better* than those of an earlier age? But this begs the question, because we are trying to find out which standards *are* better, and why. Do we seriously mean to assert that society's standards are always improving, so that present standards are a little better than those of a few years ago, and vastly superior to those of a century or more ago? Is there always a general improvement in the standards of society, even though a spot check may reveal a bit of backsliding here and there (e.g., Auschwitz)? But how do we *judge* the standards of a society, so that we may identify and praise the improvement and condemn the backsliding? Until this question is answered, the only thing we can say about contemporary standards is that they are more contemporary— hardly an enlightening discovery.

Finally, there is a third question. It is obvious that in accepting the standards of one society, I must reject those of others. But on what grounds do I do this? Do I do it on the basis of *conscience?* This would imply that it is a good thing to follow my conscience, but does this mean that I should never oppose another who is following his/her conscience, even if he/she is doing something which is, in my judgment (and in the judgment of most people), extremely harmful to myself or others (such as the running of extermination camps)? In cases of conflict, whose conscience is to prevail? Must I follow mine, simply on the grounds that it is *mine?* If so, the Auschwitz principle prevails again.

It seems clear that for all of us, the only way out of this

impasse is to admit that there is an obligation that is deeper and more serious than that of *following* conscience (in the sense of "my perception of what is right and wrong"). This deeper obligation is that of doing everything which is reasonably in my power to insure that my conscience is correct, that my perception of what is worthy or unworthy of being chosen corresponds to what is really the case, regardless of my wishes, likes, or feelings. Unless there are some ways of acting which *in and of themselves, regardless of who knows it and likes it, are worthy of being chosen, and others which are not,* unless there are values which are there, objectively, quite independently of us, no morally good decisions can ever be made. The multiple ambiguities of "doing what we feel is right" can be resolved in only two ways: either we agree that there are ways of acting which, in and of themselves, are worthy of being chosen (and others which are unworthy), whether we admit it, like it, or even know it, *or* we must admit that in finding fault with Auschwitz (which stands here for all of the inhumanity human beings have been inflicting on each other from the beginning), we have no coherent arguments at our disposal.

2.24 Summary on Situation Ethics

None of the questions with which this chapter began have been answered, but we have seen that there is one condition which must be fulfilled if *any* of these questions are ever going to be answered, and that unless that condition is fulfilled, it is foolish even to raise the questions. The condition is this: there must be ways of acting which are worthy of being chosen and others which are not, and this "worthiness" must come from the character or nature of the actions *in themselves,* and cannot depend on what any of us, individually or in groups, large or small, believe to be true, or would like to be true. Now that this condition has been stated, we can begin to answer the questions which were raised at the beginning of this chapter.

2.3 THE GREAT PARADOX

2.31 Internal and External Acts

As we try to understand the words "right" and "wrong," it is important to note that only a limited number of things we do can be described in this way. In fact, most of our actions are neither right nor wrong, neither morally good nor morally bad. In the course of a day, a year, a life, we do many things. We eat and we sleep and we dream; we help others and we hurt them; we deliberate and we slide; we cogitate and we vegetate. Common sense suggests that those things which we do *without intent,* and which therefore are not really under our control, are not properly called "right" or "wrong." Dreaming, digesting food, falling down a flight of stairs—these are all things which, in a sense, we *do,* but they are hardly things which make us good or bad persons (although in other respects, and not from the moral viewpoint, some of these actions and events could rightly be called "good" and others "bad"). Even a brief reflection shows that this common-sense judgment is sound. The only acts which can be called "right" or "wrong" are those for which we bear some degree of responsibility, because we *choose* them. These are the acts which are called, in the strict sense of the word, *moral* acts.

Note something a bit unusual in the terminology here: the word "moral" in this usage is not opposed to "immoral" but to "amoral" (not capable of being called either "right" or "wrong"). That is, the term "moral act" includes actions which are morally good as well as those which are morally bad, and only our decisions can be moral acts in this sense. When we make decisions, we are confronted with real alternatives and we are aware of them, and we freely select one and reject the other(s). It is quite appropriate that only decisions be called "good" or "bad" in the deepest sense (that is, *morally* good or bad) for a very good reason: intelligence and the freedom which is consequent on it are *distinctive* of the human animal; it is in this sector of life that we are called to be creative, and it is here that we are responsible for success and for failure.

Note again something extremely important here: our decisions, and these alone, are the *only* acts which can be called "good" or "bad" (in the moral sense), and these decisions are *internal, mental* acts. The conclusion to be drawn from this may seem strange, but it is inescapable: the things which we do, visibly and externally, to implement our choices and translate them into action—in short, *actions,* as we commonly understand the word—are not *in themselves* morally good or morally bad. When we think or speak of an action, apart from the knowledge and intent of the one who does it, and when we describe such an action, we should not use the words "right" or "wrong," and we should not use the words "good" or "bad," if what we mean is "morally good" and "morally bad." There are no morally good or morally bad actions "out there," outside of and apart from the knowledge and freedom of the individual human being; there are no virtuous acts and there are no sins *outside us.* Sin and virtue are real, as are moral good and moral evil, but they are real *in* human intelligence and intent, and not outside them. This point cannot be too strongly emphasized: the external and visible actions which follow upon our decisions are not *in themselves* moral. The practice of "defining sins," from the pulpit or elsewhere (that is, the practice of declaring that some particular action is "a serious sin"), is a bad mistake, and it will seriously hamper the effort to think clearly in moral matters.

It is perfectly correct to point out that the actions of human beings are not abstract but very concrete, and that such actions are often the consequences of decisions or choices which have been made (at least in the sense of the decision to "let things slide" or to "let nature take its course"). In such cases we can speak of the choice or decision as forming one concrete global reality with the action which results from it; but even here, the *moral* quality of the act (whether it is good or evil) comes immediately from the *intention* of the agent.

2.32 Compounding the Paradox

Does this mean that "only good intentions count" and that what we actually choose and do is of little importance? Nothing could be farther from the truth. Paradoxical as it may seem, despite the fact that our external actions follow upon our decisions, they nevertheless have the most important and serious effects on our decisions; and they have these effects precisely insofar as they are *foreseen.*

The solution to this paradox lies in the fact that in matters which we feel to be serious, we very rarely act on the basis of one single decision; rather, we usually act at the end of a series of decisions. The first of these decisions may be very hesitant and tentative—somewhat in the nature of an experiment to see how we feel when we have committed ourselves to a course of action. As we think about what we are planning to do, we may become more committed, more deeply involved, or we may become less involved, to the point of reversing the original decision. I may, for example, have a somewhat theoretical awareness of the cruelty and inhumanity involved in choosing to end the life of an innocent person or in destroying the good name and reputation of one who has done nothing to deserve this; and I may be aware of these factors when I decide to embark on just such a course of action. However, as the time to perform the action in question approaches, I will inevitably become more aware of what the action really involves, so that my knowledge becomes *real* rather than merely *notional.* Previously, my consent might have been fleeting, limited, partial. But if I continue to give this assent as the action becomes imminent, my consent will become stable, general, total. In this way, the external action, *precisely as foreseen,* can have a great effect on a decision, right up to the time at which the action is performed.

2.4 SOME VERY GOOD QUESTIONS WHICH SHOULD NOT BE CONFUSED

There are three extremely important questions which we can ask about human behavior. The first we have seen: Are there ways of acting which are worthy of being chosen, regardless of who knows it and likes it? The second is this: How do we *know* what these ways of acting are? Who decides? And the third is this: When we choose ways of acting which are objectively unworthy of being chosen, are we guilty of moral evil? Have we actually made morally bad decisions, and have we committed sin? These questions are all excellent, and they are interrelated, but, most important of all, they are *distinct* and they should not be confused.

The first question received a preliminary answer in the comments on situation ethics above: to be human is to be able to know the truth, to recognize values which are there or can be there, and to opt for ways of fostering and promoting those values. Unless such values exist, it is impossible to be human and, perhaps more to the point here, the second and third questions *would make no sense*. It is worth raising questions about how we discover values and about our responsibility for such a discovery *only if the values are there to be discovered.*

Of course the fact that there are such ways of acting does not imply that it is an easy matter to discover them, and this leads us to the second question: Who decides which ways of acting are worthy of being chosen and which are unworthy? The answer to this question is best left for the next chapter, but one point must be underlined again here: the fact that this is a question which is often answered inadequately, because it is not easy to answer it well, is no excuse for abandoning the search for values or for denying that they exist objectively.

The third question is also a very good one: Are those who perform actions which are not worthy of being chosen guilty of sin? Are they acting in a morally bad way? The only answer we can give is a provisional one: "They *may* be, but unless we know something about the knowledge and intentions of the individual involved, we have *no way of knowing for certain.*"

As we will see in the final sections of this chapter, our morally good and morally bad acts have both objective components (facts and events in the world outside and around us), and subjective components (which have real existence in our minds and in our acts of understanding and intending). If the questions listed in §2.4 above are understood and kept distinct, we can do justice to both the objective and the subjective elements of our moral lives; otherwise this will be impossible.

2.5 RESPONSIBILITY AND ITS LIMITATIONS

We have emphasized that only our decisions can be called morally good or morally bad, right or wrong. But not even all of our decisions can be described in this way. For many of our apparent choices we bear no responsibility at all, while for others we are fully responsible; and there is a large gray area, where our responsibility is real but limited. These limitations of responsibility are always the result of factors which remove certain elements of a situation from the control of free choice. Moral theologians have often listed under three headings the factors which limit human responsibility: inattention, ignorance, and force.

2.51 Inattention or Lack of Awareness

If we are not really conscious, then we are not capable of free activity and obviously cannot make a choice. If we are sleepwalking, drugged, or drunk, our understanding of the possibilities in a situation will be at the very least limited, and possibly entirely absent. (In all of these cases, we will have to raise the question, later, of whether we entered these various states of diminished consciousness *voluntarily,* if we chose them freely. If we did, then it will be *that choice*—the unwillingness to prevent loss of control over our actions—which *may* have to be judged morally bad.) If I am daydreaming while at the wheel of my car and accidentally kill a pedestrian, I certainly am not guilty of intending to kill an innocent person. But, depending on other factors, I may have done something seriously wrong in allowing my attention to wander.

2.52 Ignorance

A second factor which can limit responsibility is ignorance. Here this word has a sense somewhat out of the ordinary, and means *the absence of knowledge which in some way it would be desirable for us to have.* We can freely choose a course of action only when we know what the alternatives are, and what at least the more important effects will be, and therefore, when this knowledge is absent, the "choice" may not be really free at all, at least in respect to a particular effect (that is, it may not be a *choice* in the proper sense). But here again we may ask whether we are, at times, *responsible for the ignorance itself.* Moral theologians have dealt with this question by distinguishing two kinds of ignorance—vincible and invincible.

Invincible ignorance is not an unfortunate mental state which cannot be remedied even by the efforts of the most dedicated teachers. It is merely the absence of knowledge which, for some reason, it would be desirable for me to have (at least in the sense that harm would be avoided), but which, for practical reasons, I do not have *and cannot be reasonably expected to have.* An example will illustrate this point. Let us assume that I take reasonably good care of my car, but that, despite this fact, one day my brakes fail, and I crash into the back of the car in front of me, injuring some of the passengers. Let us also assume that if I had made an exhaustive check of the hydraulic system before I drove off that day, I would have spotted the difficulty and been able to prevent the accident. Despite this latter fact, my ignorance of the state of the brake system when I drove off has to be called *invincible,* because in *practical* terms it was irremediable. It would be *unreasonable* to demand that I subject my car to an exhaustive mechanical check-up every time I drive it. (Very different, of course, would be the case if I were driving a car which I knew was not roadworthy; here I would be consciously and culpably using a deadly weapon which I will very likely not be able to control, and my *willingness* to act in this way is morally wrong and seriously so.) Note, by the way, that what is under discussion here is *moral* responsibility, not *legal* responsibility. The law deals primarily and directly with externally verifiable actions, and with the liability which one incurs in performing or omitting them. One may be legally responsible for something without being morally guilty, and one may also be free of legal responsibility while being morally culpable.

The other type of ignorance is called *vincible* and it refers to the absence of knowledge which it would be desirable for me to have, and which *I can reasonably be expected to have*. I could acquire the knowledge in question *by taking ordinary, prudent, reasonable* steps. A simple example will illustrate this. Let us assume that I have parked my car on a steep hill and then gotten out of the car and walked about a block. Suddenly I realize that I do not remember setting the emergency brake. I am uncertain, and, in the sense in which we are using the word here, I am *ignorant* of whether or not the brake is set. Now if the car were later to start down the hill on its own and kill a pedestrian at the intersection, I would certainly not be guilty of the decision or intention to kill a pedestrian; however, neither would I be free of moral guilt. Not only is certainty about whether the hand brake had been set a bit of knowledge which it would be desirable for me to have; it is also knowledge which I can acquire very easily by the simple expedient of walking back to the car and checking whether or not the brake has been set. My ignorance here is *vincible* because it can be removed by taking a simple, prudent, *reasonable* course of action. Jurisprudence is also aware of vincible ignorance, although it employs a different term. The law makes use of the concept of negligence here and implies that we have the obligation to be informed about the effects of our actions, and to act in a reasonable way when the rights of others are involved.

As a final point, note this: the line between the two kinds of ignorance is a bit fuzzy for two reasons. First, there will always be cases in which we have to ask if enough time and energy were spent in attempting to discover the real nature of the choices we had to make, and therefore if a small degree of negligence might have been involved. Second, political and social conditions may make knowledge in certain areas virtually impossible to attain at certain times in history. It is here that such factors as the *consensus of our contemporaries* or *contemporary standards* have an important role to play in determining our responsibility. These factors have *no effect whatsoever* on the objective worthiness or unworthiness of a given way of acting, but they may greatly limit our power *to see, to be aware of* this worthiness or unworthiness. As we will note in the rest of this book, it is always a good thing to work for the elimination of ignorance, but there are limits to what can be accomplished at any given moment of history. And remember that ignorance can extend not only to the facts of a given situation, but, even more importantly, to matters of *principle*—that is, to the question of what issues are really at stake in the choices we are called upon to make.

2.53 Force

A third factor which can limit responsibility is force. Some kinds of force obviously prevent an apparent decision from being a real decision at all. Physical force can put me in a situation which is not of my own choosing—I may be forced at gunpoint to participate in a bank robbery, and the fact that the gun is on me prevents the participation from being an act of choice at all. What is usually involved in such cases is mental or psychological pressure; fear, anxiety, anger, desire, will normally lessen, and at times even eliminate, responsibility for actions which are performed under their influence. (Even civil law recognizes this, and speaks of either temporary insanity, extreme provocation, or diminished responsibility.) As we will see later, sometimes the "decisions" which we seem to make under the influence of these strong psychological pressures are not really decisions at all. But we still have to ask this question: Was there a decision (at least in the sense of a *willingness*) involved in allowing these pressures to build up to the point at which they became irresistible? If I give free rein to my anger, it may well build up to the point at which I will behave in a literally irresponsible way—that is, without responsibility—but it is possible that there were important elements of choice involved *precisely in allowing this to happen,* and therefore that I was to some degree responsible for precisely that. Strong emotion, whether in the form of fear, anger, or desire, may rob me of my power to make a free choice in a given matter, but I may well be responsible for allowing myself to get into a situation where this will happen. (This is the question which was traditionally discussed under the heading "occasions of sin.")

The use of mind-altering drugs, heavy drinking, the lack of any attempt at emotional control, are undesirable actions for this reason: we *ought* to be able to make intelligent and free choices as we go through life. But note this: the degree to which we are responsible for our decisions will depend on the degree to which we *should* have knowledge of ourselves and of the situation in which we find ourselves. This may vary with age, with our state of physical and mental health, with our maturity, with our mental ability, and with many other factors. This suggests a point of cardinal importance which we will develop later: *our basic responsibility is to act in an informed and intelligent way.* We are responsible for opening the issues to examination, but we often try to avoid this responsibility out of the guilty suspicion that, if we examined the evidence, we could not continue to act as we please—that is, in an *irresponsible* way.

2.54 Some Problems with This Approach

This way of speaking of factors which limit our responsibility is traditional, and by no means unsound; but at times in the past it has been applied in a somewhat mechanical way, and this has caused problems. Some moral theologians devoted all of their attention to *individual actions* and did not give enough thought to the question of the good and virtuous *life*. Recently, and as a corrective to this, moral theologians have emphasized that *character* and *responsibility* should be stressed more than the individual act. They have pointed out that a moral theory which concentrates on individual actions can easily become a morality of *law,* and that this leads inevitably to minimalism (how much can I get away with before I violate the law?).

Much in this objection is valid, but in the attempt to provide a remedy, some have spoken as though character, one's habitual stance, counted for everything, while one's individual actions were unimportant. But this way of speaking is inaccurate; it is a good example of confused thinking, and it will lead to more of the same. Good character and a generally responsible stance toward a morally good life should not be contrasted with or pitted against individual moral acts. The problem was not precisely that moral theologians were concentrating on actions to the detriment of character and responsibility, but rather that, at least at times, they were concentrating on *the wrong actions.* Sometimes these theologians seemed to forget that *decisions* and not *external actions* were the only things to which the terms "morally good" and "morally bad" could be applied.

Even more frequently, they seemed to be concerned with that decision which immediately preceded the external, perceivable action. In other words, they oversimplified, and they often spoke as though there were just one real decision behind every action.

But the decision-making process is much more complicated than this, and in matters which we sense to be important, each action is preceded by many decisions (perhaps hundreds in some cases). Some of these earlier decisions are hesitant and tentative, but others are not, and it is often these decisions which take place at some distance in time from the final action that *form character, fashion the responsible self, and create the real person.* Particularly important, as we will see, are those decisions in which we choose to remain open to facts which we would like to suppress, to evidence which we do not feel like admitting to the discussion, and to the truth which we perceive as a threat to the comfortable existence which we have made for ourselves. (And, of course, equally important are those decisions in which we blind ourselves to these facts, this evidence, this truth.) But remember that these decisions, although not external, visible actions, are still actions, and they are precisely the actions with which moral theology must concern itself. It is our concern for character and responsibility which demands that we pay a great deal of attention to these actions; unless we do, talk about the importance of character and responsibility is nothing more than a particularly repulsive variety of psychobabble.

A second problem with traditional reflection on factors limiting responsibility was a consequence of the idea of freedom which many of its exponents presupposed. The moral act was thought to have distinct prerequisites in the intellect and the will, and these were conceived of as two distinct "faculties" or pigeon-holes in the mind. The task of the intellect was to present alternatives to the will, which could then act or not act, act in one way or the other. Freedom was then defined precisely in terms of this indifference, this "not-being-determined-by-anything-outside-itself," which was supposed to be a characteristic of the will. And it was this definition of freedom which led to the view which is most common today: the view that we are free if not coerced, and therefore that freedom consists in being able to do whatever we want or please.

But this view is an impoverishment of freedom. Our most basic decision, and the one we are in the process of making all of the days of our lives, is the *decision to be free or unfree.* The decision to be free is the decision to be *receptive to reality and to the demands which it makes upon us.* We are free when we willingly act in an intelligent way. Of course freedom can also be thought of as a *power,* in virtue of which we *can* act, and then it should be defined as the power or capacity to choose the truly intelligent way of acting. Any number of problems concerning freedom and its apparent conflicts with either the omnipotence of God or with the various coercive factors in the human situation can be dealt with effectively if we accept and understand this definition.

2.55 The Question of Limited Responsibility: A Summary

We can summarize our approach to the question of which of our actions are properly called "right" or "wrong" in the following way. *First,* only our decisions can be properly called "right" or "wrong" in the moral sense. It is neither useful nor accurate to use these words in speaking of our *external, visible* actions. The act of bringing about the death of an innocent person can be called many things, but it should not be called "wrong" or "morally bad." The act of visiting the sick can be called many things, but it should not be called "morally good." The *decision* to commit murder can be called "morally bad" and the *decision* to visit the sick can be called "morally good." Some moral theologians would like to speak of the decision and the action as forming a unity, a whole, and therefore they like to speak of this "whole" as morally good or bad, but this way of speaking creates unnecessary confusion and makes it very difficult to think and speak intelligently about moral questions.

Second, we can make decisions only when we are aware of the real alternatives involved, and the decisions which we make are always a choice among alternatives *insofar as we are aware of them.* These alternatives exist because different courses of action are desirable in different respects. There are many factors which can influence the desirability of the alternatives, or even the *presence* of the alternatives. Panic, fear, complete ignorance of certain facts—all of these can place us, at least momentarily, in situations in which there are really no alternatives, and in which a free decision is for that reason not possible. This is particularly true of initial reactions to a panic situation. At the instant at which my car strikes a pedestrian, I may be able to think only of getting away from this shattering event as quickly as possible. But in a moment, other factors will come to mind: the injured human being in need of help, my own integrity and self-respect, the harm which will come to my family if I am caught. In the face of these alternatives, I become capable of making a decision.

The situations which were mentioned above under the heading of invincible ignorance could well be reexamined here. When they are, it becomes clear that when our ignorance is invincible, there are no real alternatives, and therefore there are no decisions. But the question, of course, which must always be raised in such cases is this: At some earlier moment should I have taken steps to remedy my ignorance? *Should* I be able to see other alternatives in this situation? Was there something which I did or did not do at an earlier stage which makes it difficult or impossible for me to see what the real alternatives are now?

In the *third* place, a morally good or bad act is one in which we are aware that our decision in favor of one of the alternatives is one which we *should* or *should not* make. Later sections of this book will go into the question of what it is which endows some decisions with this quality, and for the moment it is enough to note that there are many factors which can keep us from being aware that the alternatives have this "should" or "should not" character. Contemporary standards—the values of most people at the time at which we live, or the standards of our social class or peer group—can be very influential here. If these standards are incorrect, they can prevent us from knowing that a certain decision is one which we should or should not make. Again, our views of right and wrong may be distorted because of *character defects.* We may be responsible, at least partially, for these defects, and we may have these defects because of bad decisions which we made in the past. If so, we are responsible for those *past bad decisions.* But it may also be true that, at least at the present moment, our decisions in some matters are only marginally moral, if at all. Finally, it may be true that because of some neurotic twist, some factor which inhibited our growth to moral maturity, we remain *moral infants,* really incapable of seeing that element of "should" or "should not" which faces us in some of our decisions. Just as there are some whose intellectual growth stops at the age of two, five, or ten, there are some whose moral growth stops at similar points.

The *fourth* point in our summary on the question of which acts can be called morally good or morally bad is more in the nature of a comment. It seems clear that the essential element in the moral act is *awareness*—both of the existence of the alternatives and of the moral quality of these alternatives (that is, whether they *should* or *should not* be chosen). From this it seems clear that we can be *partially* responsible for our decisions, and that this may often be the case.

This would be a good time to emphasize something hinted at earlier. In much that we do, the really significant moral acts occur at a much earlier stage than do the *apparent* decisions. (These significant moral acts are, of course, decisions, but they are often, erroneously, not seen to be decisions.) As we have seen, when emotional reactions are strong, the final "decision" may be only marginally moral. In a moment of panic, we may be incapable of making any decision at all, but as the panic lessens, we will become increasingly responsible, as alternatives (re)appear, and as our awareness of their moral qualification awakens. On the contrary, when we are dealing with the deliberate, planned, "cold-blooded" act (for example, murder of an innocent person), when the external action draws near, our responsibility for our decision is likely to grow, because decisions which reaffirm the original option are continually being made in the face of the ever more evident unworthiness of such a way of acting. As we suggested above, it is often at moments of life when we have the opportunity to *anticipate* problems before they occur, to *fashion sound policy* before the moment of crisis arrives, to *commit ourselves firmly to a worthy ideal before we are blinded by the pressures of the situation*—it is often at such moments of life that moral decisions of great importance are made.

2.6 RESOLVING THE PARADOXES

2.61 Apparently Conflicting Demands

Morally good and morally bad decisions are made by human beings, human subjects, and they deal with events and facts in the real world—events which are already real, or which can become real if we want them to. There are obviously *objective* elements in our decision-making, because we have to take note of what is really there, confronting us with the task of making a choice. And there are also subjective elements, because we are human subjects (which means simply that *we* are the ones who are doing the thinking and the intending). Both sides of the decision-making process are quite real, and we have to do justice to both. We have to recognize that the same real world is "out there," confronting all of us with its possibilities and its demands—in short, with its *reality*. But we have to recognize that each one of us is absolutely *unique*—not exactly like anyone else who has ever lived or ever will.

It is extremely important to see that these two facets of decision-making are not in competition, and that our task is not to find some "golden mean" between them, or to balance them, and then sum up our efforts with some pretentious platitude about "keeping both aspects of the question in view at all times." Our task is to identify precisely what the objective element of decision-making consists in, and then to affirm that objectivity in the most uncompromising terms. And our task is to do the same with the subjective element.

2.62 The Objective Element in Our Moral Decisions

The objective element which is always present in the moral decision can be simply stated: in every concrete and unique situation in which we find ourselves, there are objective values which stand in a *real* relation of relative importance and which therefore make *real* and objective demands on us. The judgments which we make about such situations will be either true or false (and can be so in varying degrees) and their truth or falsity depends on whether or not they do justice to the objective situation.

2.63 The Subjective Side of Decision-Making

If we are clear about this fact, then there is no difficulty in admitting that the views of society, the opinions of men and women of good will, the limitations imposed by the historical epoch in which we live, all play a very important role in decision-making. But these various conditioning factors do *not* determine whether ways of acting in themselves are valuable or not. They have no effect whatsoever on the reality of value and its presence in a concrete situation. What they do affect (and often limit) is our *ability to perceive* the values which are there. We are to a great extent dependent on others for our perception of value (to a greater degree than we like to admit), and if others have failed in their responsibility to us, we may make many errors in judgment about value, for which we bear little or no responsibility. (And, of course, we may bear much of the responsibility for the erroneous judgments of others, if we have failed in our responsibility to them.) In the same way, we are affected by the *mores*, the habitual moral judgments, which are current in the civilization and culture in which we live our lives. Often these judgments carry such a weight of numbers and of history that it is difficult for the individual to prevail against them. This does not mean that it is a morally good or even tolerable thing for an individual to simply accept the bad moral judgments of a majority; it does mean that under the pervasive influence of moral judgments held by almost all of those whom we know and respect, it can be extremely difficult to make correct judgments about the objective values which are really or potentially present in a concrete situation.

The conviction of the objectivity of moral value is the only basis on which a meaningful ethical system can be built. In the absence of this conviction, we human beings become warped parodies of ourselves, and all talk of acting rightly or wrongly becomes an exercise in futility. It is quite true that there is something unique about every situation in which we are called to make a decision, and it is true that these situations cannot be typed or classified so accurately that decision-making could be reduced to the application of general norms or rules of conduct to specific cases. No ethical system should ever deny this. But there is an objective element in every unique situation, and it consists in the fact that the values, personal and material, about which we are called to decide *are objectively real,* and stand in a network of relationships which are *there,* whether we like it or not. And no ethical system should ever deny this either.

If we are clear about this fact, then we can afford to be honest about the difficulties which we almost always encounter when we try to discover these values, and we can be tolerant of the failure of ourselves and others to discover these values and to implement them. But at the same time we can approach these failures with confidence, and with the conviction that it is worth trying again and again to discover these elusive values.

It is time to turn now to a question which has been waiting in the wings impatiently for some time: Which ways of acting *are* objectively worthy of being chosen, and which are objectively unworthy? How do we find out? Who can make such a decision? And who is worth listening to when he or she decides? This is really the question of the norm or standard of morality, and answering this question will be the work of the following chapter.

3

The Problem
of Moral Norms

In raising the question of what the words "right" and "wrong" mean when applied to human actions, we have talked about ways of acting which are "worthy (or unworthy) of being chosen." This is a rather cumbersome and even clumsy way of speaking about actions which have traditionally been called "good" or "bad" in the sense of *morally good* or *morally bad*. However, we have avoided the simpler and, at first sight, clearer terms deliberately, and for good reason. To talk about actions themselves as "right" or "wrong," "good" or "bad" (in the moral sense), apart from the concrete circumstances in which they occur, and apart from the intentions of the concrete human beings performing them, is a serious mistake, *precisely because it makes the defense of the objectivity of value extremely difficult;* but more of this later.

3.1 THE SOURCE OF THE "WORTHINESS" OR "UNWORTHINESS" OF OUR ACTIONS

Why are some ways of acting worthy of being chosen and why are other ways of acting unworthy of being chosen? Each of these questions implies two further questions. First, what is the ground or basis, in the world "out there" which we confront, for this "worthiness" or "unworthiness" of some of our actions? And second, how can we make *correct judgments* about this "worthiness" or "unworthiness"?

The implications of this last question are important: we are *called on* to make correct judgments about the worthiness or unworthiness of different ways of acting and we have an obligation to be *judgmental*—a stance which will certainly not endear us to the defenders of situation ethics. The word "judgmental," of course, can mean two different things, and it is true that we are not called upon to make judgments about the moral guilt or innocence of other persons nor are we called upon to accuse them of committing sin. On the other hand we *are* called upon to do our best to make correct judgments about which ways of acting are *in themselves* worthy of being chosen. In fact, *to refuse to be judgmental in the second sense is a most serious assault on the objectivity of value* and it is a regression to the Auschwitz principle of morality.

3.2 WHAT ARE MORAL NORMS AND HOW DO THEY FUNCTION?

In attempting to discover which ways of acting are, *in themselves,* worthy of being chosen and which are not, it will be best to start with the question of how we make such judgments. This is the question which is usually treated under the heading of the *norm(s) of morality,* but it will be easier to understand norms of morality by turning first to other kinds of norms which we encounter in everyday life.

In the simplest terms, a norm is a measuring stick or a

standard with which we can compare some object or process to determine whether it has the qualities and characteristics which it "ought" to have or "should" have. For example, in most countries, standard measures (foot, yard, gallon, liter, meter, etc.) are kept under controlled conditions of temperature and humidity in a government laboratory, and they serve as the ultimate norm or standard with which other measuring sticks can be compared for accuracy.

3.21 Norms and Ideals

One way of looking at a norm is to see it as an *ideal*—a desirable shape, size, way of acting, against which we can compare objects or projected ways of acting and make judgments like these: "quite close to the ideal," "falls far short of the ideal," etc. It is a short step from speaking of a desirable (or undesirable) shape, size, or way of acting, to speaking of things which are "good" and "bad," "right" and "wrong." Often, instead of making complicated statements about the degree of approximation to an ideal, we simply say that a thing or action is "good" or "bad" (or "not so good," "poor"). In other words, we use the words "good" and "bad" (or the equivalent) in many matters which have *nothing to do* with ethics or morality. And if we pay careful attention to this use of the words "good" and "bad," we will be able to learn something about the way the words are used in moral and ethical matters.

3.22 The Relationship of Norms, Ideals, and Purposes

The point is so important that it is worth repeating. We use the words "good" and "bad" to speak of many things, objects, events, and actions, which are part of our everyday lives, and we use them, most of the time, without intending to make moral judgments at all. For example, we can speak of good cars, good cigarettes, good jobs, good books, good movies, good music, good investments, good theories. In all of these cases, the word "good" implies that the action or thing in question *does what it should do*, attains its *purpose*, fulfills the end or goal which is proper to it. If I think that a car should provide cheap and comfortable transportation, then a good car is one which will do just that. The fact that the car in question does not impress the neighbors or build up my ego does not make it a bad car, because, presumably, I do not think that these are things which a car should be called upon to do. In the same way, a good cigarette is supposed to taste like a cigarette should, or perhaps have a minimum of carcinogenic tars. If one or the other of these qualities is first on the list of things which I expect from a cigarette, then I will not call any cigarette "good" which fails to pass the test in question. Similarly, a good movie should, depending on my tastes and expectations, inform me, illuminate the meaning of life for me, or simply entertain me. A good stereo is one which fulfills the purpose of a piece of high fidelity equipment: it duplicates (or perhaps even improves on!) the original live performance. A good theory will provide either a valid explanation of the data, or a useful model which will help me understand the data. Good jobs, good music, good investments— all of these will be "good" if they attain the *ends* and *purposes* proper to them, and we will call them "bad" or "no good" if they do not attain these ends, at least as we see them.

We can summarize the relationship of norms, purposes, and ideals this way: we create norms in order to determine whether things fulfill their purposes or not. A norm is an ideal, expressed in the form of a judgment, which enables us to make further practical judgments about things or actions. When we judge objects or actions according to their ability to attain one or another purpose, what we are really doing is *specifying the qualities that product or action should have if it is to attain its goal most effectively.* If the purpose of a car is to provide cheap and reliable transportation, then it should be fuel-efficient, have a good frequency-of-repair record, and when repairs are needed, they should be capable of being performed easily and cheaply. These qualities or characteristics are the *norms* or *standards* we will keep in mind when we go to buy a car. In a similar way, the purpose of the game of golf is to go around the course, using the minimum number of strokes to put the ball in eighteen successive holes. We will attain this goal if we hit long, straight drives, accurate approach shots, and deadly putts, and therefore these aspects of the game are the norms or standards we apply when asked to judge the golfing abilities of ourselves or of others. Whenever we use the words "good" and "bad," we are judging something or someone by measuring it (or them) in accordance with some norm or standard (and this norm or standard is derived, in turn, from the purpose of that thing or person). This is an insight of key importance as we try to determine what the words "good" and "bad," "right" and "wrong" mean when we apply them to moral matters.

These examples show something else which is quite important. To some extent, things have their own inherent, natural ends—here the word "natural" means simply "as common sense would see it." But at the same time, most things have a certain plasticity or malleability—they can achieve different ends, fulfill different purposes, and to some degree we can determine the goals or purposes which we want them to fulfill. Usually this happens without destroying the inherent or "natural" purpose of a thing, although it may happen that the latter purpose is pushed out of first place. For example, we might say that a car is in it-self, inherently, a means of transportation, but while serv-ing as such, it may also be a status symbol (direct or inverse), an index of wealth, compensation for an inferiority com-plex, or an expensive toy with which I play. It is even possible that the car might stop being a means of transpor-tation, and become an object with which I tinker, either for relaxation or for training.

3.23 The Status of Norms: Where Do They Come From?

One point should be noted here: these norms or stan-dards do not exist "out there," apart from the critical, judg-ing faculties of human beings. This is not to assert that such norms are purely subjective, or that they are figments of the imagination. Rather, they are *ways of thinking* about *real things,* about their purposes, and about effective ways of at-taining those purposes. They are tools which we use to de-termine whether things are attaining their purposes or not. (Norms, in the sense of "judgments which other individuals or groups have made" may pre-exist any individual person, but they do not exist outside and apart from human beings; they are precisely the judgments which are made by some individual or group. This is what it means to speak of "norms of society"; in themselves, they are normative for those who make them, and for no one else.) Norms and standards are constructions, creations of human intelligence, and we make them on the basis of ob-servation and analysis of the real world. There are truly ob-jective elements which stand behind all norms and standards, precisely because they are judgments about *ob-jectively real values,* and these judgments will be either cor-rect or incorrect, true or false (or partially so).

3.3 "GOOD" AND "BAD", "RIGHT" AND "WRONG" IN THE MORAL SENSE

In talking about norms and ideals, and in judging ways of attaining the various purposes they imply, we have been talking about *partial and limited* purposes in life. Golf games, stereos, cars, and computers are all "good" or "bad" from one or another point of view, and in terms of attaining purposes *which we determine* (within some very broad limits). In all of these cases, we have been talking about the purposes of *things* that we have invented, and which are products of our technology or of our playfulness.

We can go a step further and talk about our goals and purposes for life as a whole. And as soon as we do this, it becomes evident that we have many such goals. We expect many things from life, and we approach each day with many hopes. We all want *happiness,* but each of us defines this in terms of a unique combination of security, joy, peace, power, pleasure, diversion, receiving, and giving. In varying degrees, these are our goals in life, and we measure our actions by their efficacy in helping us to attain these goals. But the obvious problem is that an action may be "good" in terms of one of these goals (that is, very helpful in attaining it), and may not be at all good (or may even be very "bad") in terms of another of these goals because it interferes with attaining it. A well-paying but boring job would be a good example here: "good" from the standpoint of financial security, but "bad" from the standpoint of personal satisfaction. On a deeper level, some actions which will give us great power over things and persons will at the same time rob us of our inner peace. But even on this deeper level, we are still talking about partial and limited goals of life.

3.31 A Deeper Question

The discussion of the partial and limited purposes of the things we make and use, of our jobs and our pleasures, our plans and our commitments, might suggest another question. Does human life as a whole have a purpose? Is there an over-all goal of human life? Can we speak of an ideal human life and construct a picture of the kind of life which would attain the human goal? If this were the case, we could judge any particular form of human conduct by asking whether it helps us to attain our purpose as human beings or whether it interferes with this purpose. Is there any way an action can be good, not merely in terms of one or another of these subordinate purposes and goals of human life, but simply in terms of human life, human existence *itself*? If there were, it would be possible to resolve these conflicts among the various goals of life, and it would be possible to speak of some decisions as *simply* "good" or *simply* "bad." We could speak of these decisions, not in terms of ends or goals *which we assign*, but in terms of the end or goal which we have as human beings, and which *we have not assigned or chosen*, but which has been given to us. This question indicates how it might be possible to describe some patterns of action, some ways of acting, as "good" (because they are conducive to the end or goal of human life) and others as "bad" (because they frustrate the attainment of this goal). Note that in this case, we are using the words "good" and "bad" in the usual way, to describe the connection of something with its goal or purpose. But at the same time, we are using them in a *special* way, because we are not talking about some partial or subordinate purpose of life (for example, buying a cheap means of transportation, or devising a scientific theory), but rather about the all-embracing purpose of life, and therefore we are talking, not about actions which are "good" or "bad" from some particular point of view, but about actions which are "good" or "bad" for us *as human beings,* as persons. Furthermore, if there is an over-all purpose for human life, the implication is that this purpose is given in the nature of the case and is not ours to determine. The implication is that such a goal or purpose claims us, not simply as golfers or as stereo aficionados, but as human beings. If we used the words "good" and "bad," "right" and "wrong" in speaking of such ways of acting, then we would be speaking of *moral* good and *moral* evil.

3.32 But Does Life Have Such a Unique Goal?

Does it make any sense to talk about *the* purpose or goal of human life, as though there were only one? Is it really possible to construct a norm or standard for the good human life? Does human existence have such a goal or purpose which is the same for all of us and for each of us? Disagreement about how this question should be answered is the greatest single problem of philosophical and theological ethics. But it is good to keep two things in mind. First, this is not simply a question for ethics or theology. It is a universally human question. And one of the most fascinating ways of understanding an historical period is to inquire about that period's conception of the ideal person—that is, to ask about the kind of human existence which is normative for such a society and which is regarded as a standard by which the lives of all men and women may be judged. Second, remember that the answer to this question is given not only by philosophical and theological ethics, but in all literature, and, more generally, in all of the art forms of a given historical period. It is for this reason that literature and other forms of art have such an important place in the educational process. It is not simply a question of inculcating the proper esthetic tastes in the young, but rather of transmitting the views of society on the goals of human existence, and therefore the views of this same society on what the ideal person should be.

We might ask at this point if Christian faith, relying on revelation (basically, the Old and New Testaments), and perhaps on the teaching of Church authorities, does not provide us with a view of human existence and with the means of understanding and acting upon it which would solve the problem, at least for Christians. This is a good question, but it will be better to delay the answer for two reasons.

First, if those who are not Christian can act rightly and well (and they certainly can and do—often in ways which should put Christians to shame), then there must be some way of speaking about the purpose and end of existence which is not restricted to Christians, and which non-Christains can understand and act upon. Since we live in a pluralistic society, in which we are called upon to act rightly and well in concert with those who do not share our faith, it is important for us to discover these ways of speaking about the purpose of life.

Second, it would be a good idea to delay the answer, because the Christian view of the purpose of existence has often been stated in rather pietistic, other-worldly terms, and it may turn out that the attempt to state the purpose of human existence in generically human rather than specifically Christian terms will be of great help in understanding the contribution which Christian faith itself makes to moral decision-making.

3.33 A Serious Problem

Over the course of history, from the earliest period in Egypt and Sumer, through Greece from Homeric times to the Golden Age of Athens, in Rome and the medieval world which was largely its heir, and up to modern times, we can trace a number of divergent and conflicting views of the human ideal which have enjoyed wide currency, and which still do today.

This brings us face to face with the single most serious problem of ethics and moral theology: people do not agree on the purposes and goals of life as a whole. Disagreement not only touches questions of golf, stereos, cars, and jobs, but it also touches questions of which ways of acting are "good" or "bad" in simply *human* terms. These differences are found among intelligent people who are, at the same time, men and women of good will, and they touch some very serious questions: questions of the value of human life itself (capital punishment, abortion); questions of the permanence, or the lack thereof, of the most fundamental human commitment (marriage and divorce); questions of the permissibility of the use of violence in individual and collective defense (nuclear deterrent forces); questions of economic and social justice (dealing with apartheid, the role of government in promoting economic justice). Furthermore, not only are there disagreements on practical questions of whether this or that way of acting promotes or interferes with the attainment of the goal and purpose of human life; in addition, there is disagreement about the overall goal of human life itself. We might be tempted to point out that such disagreement is age-old, but there is something unique about the modern problem.

3.34 The Specifically Modern Problem

Even in antiquity people were aware that very different views about the purpose of human life enjoyed wide currency, and they held strongly to some and rejected others. Jews who were serious about their Old Testament religious heritage rejected the cosmopolitan syncretism of the Hellenistic world, and Virgil made Aeneas, his epic hero, the embodiment of stern dedication to the gods, to his country, and to his family—a dedication which stands in striking contrast to the charming craftiness of Odysseus. What *is* distinctively modern is the fear that nothing can be done about these disagreements, and that no cogent and convincing arguments can be made in favor of one particular view of the purpose of human life and against all others. Relativism, the conviction that there is no such thing as absolute truth, and that all judgments of value depend on where you are standing (or that beauty is solely in the eye of the beholder) is very characteristic of the age in which we live.

In the past, partisans of a particular view of the purpose of life argued that their views alone were correct, and they often gave this conviction a religious justification, arguing that it had been revealed by God or the gods. With the decline in belief in God (or gods), in the sense of "all powerful, personal Other(s)," people have become agnostic in matters of value, as well as in matters of truth. Under the guise of the modern "virtue" of tolerance, the human race seems likely to lose the one conviction which makes us distinctively human: the conviction that there are values worth living for and (at least in some cases) worth dying for. Most Christians, at least officially, still hold an absolutist position on this question and argue that there are objective values which depend on God and God's word. But the problem is that different groups of Christians do not agree on what these values are: The National Council of Churches and the Moral Majority are at opposite ends of a very broad spectrum of irreconcilable views about ways of acting which help us to attain the human goal.

The problems posed by all of these disagreements are extremely serious, and they seem to make it impossible to formulate workable norms for the moral act which would be capable of winning broad acceptance. Even more serious is the fact that they leave those who are searching for objective values in a state of uncertainty and doubt about whether such values can be discovered and even about whether they exist or not. This is a serious problem for one very good reason: unless human existence has an end or goal which is fundamentally the same for all of us, there are no valid norms for determining which of our decisions are right and which are wrong. The picture seems bleak indeed, but there is an answer, and a very good one, if we are willing to turn to an old but much misunderstood idea which was developed by a number of Christian thinkers, and which received its most brilliant expression in the work of Thomas Aquinas in the thirteenth century. The idea is that of *natural law*.

3.4 NATURAL LAW

It is probably true to say that Thomas' own thought on the question of natural law would receive a much more sympathetic hearing today if it were not for the word "law" in the phrase. The word "law" in modern American English means "a piece or a body of legislation which specifies forms of activity which are either prescribed or forbidden, and which imposes sanctions for the violation of its directives." This understanding may be "stretched," when applied to natural law, by pointing out that creation is a kind of legislation, in which God specifies certain forms of activity as being in accord with his creative purpose, but we are really dealing with a metaphor here, and things would have been much clearer if the word "law" had been avoided in the translation. In the rest of this section, I will use the term "natural law" (with the quotes) to indicate the solid core of our tradition which, as noted, really antedates Thomas Aquinas but which received its clearest exposition in his writings.

3.41 Natural Law in the Christian Tradition

Many people today are not sympathetic to the concept of natural law, and this is partially due to the way the term was understood and used in traditional moral teaching—if not by the best minds, at least very often by the mediocre minds (who are always in the majority). As we have seen, some of the difficulties in this tradition spring from the word "law" itself, which was used in a sense quite different from that which is common in Anglo-Saxon jurisprudence. Many people who are not familiar with this tradition think that "natural law" means a set of rules which God made up in heaven, which are known only to the hierarchy of the Catholic Church, and which are invoked against anything which displeases the members of this hierarchy. It will be helpful here to examine briefly the Christian, and especially the Catholic, moral tradition on the question of moral norms and particularly on the question of "natural law," which was often referred to as the "objective moral norm."

In general, this moral tradition has given a very confident answer to the question of whether norms or standards exist by which our actions can be judged, and churchmen have branded the failure to see and acknowledge such norms as culpable ignorance. The norms were regarded as simply "there," as more or less obvious implications of a global reality called "human nature," and they were sometimes treated as though they had been inscribed on eternal tablets in heaven before the world began.

A good example of this way of thinking is afforded by what is often referred to as "the official Catholic position" on birth control or contraception. The argument usually took the following form: The sexual powers of human beings are directed toward the procreation of children. This is evident from the fact that genital sex aims at the fertilization of the ovum and from the fact that all other uses of the sexual faculties are designed to lead to genital sex. Therefore any full actuation of the sexual powers which deliberately excludes the possibility of conception is contrary to the immanent purpose of human sexuality. (Note that on its own level, and granted certain presuppositions, this reasoning is quite correct. In recent years, a number of Catholic moral theologians have come to question the traditional teaching, not because they find defects in the logic, but because they have come to question some of its presuppositions.)

The roots of this older, more traditional way of thinking about natural law lie deep, but I believe we can understand the way this tradition approached the question of norms by pointing to two factors which have characterized particularly the Catholic world-view (and most Catholic philosophy and theology) from medieval times and well into this century: this world-view was *non-historical*, and in it *law* played a predominant role, in the private as well as in the public sector of life.

This older view was non-historical because it assumed

that God had created the world once and for all at the beginning, and had imposed on everything a fixed and immutable purpose. Even when the concept of evolutionary development began to win more and more adherents, philosophers and theologians talked as though human beings themselves were untouched by the evolutionary process, and therefore remained unchanged in the midst of a changing world. According to this view, human beings possessed a stable *nature* in which permanently valid moral imperatives were rooted.

Those who shared this world-view tended to be very optimistic about the ability of men and women to reach the truth in matters of moral conduct and to be certain about the conclusions to which they came. But those who held this view paid a price for their optimism. They refused to see human nature as something which changed, grew, and developed, as something *living,* in which all of the functions and powers are constantly conditioned by all of the others. Human nature was viewed *statically*—"frozen," as it were— and, as a result, the various powers and faculties of human nature tended to be seen in isolation, and the human being was looked on as an aggregate of pigeon-holes: intellect, will, emotion, etc., each performing its separate function. Finally, the isolation of the faculties from each other, and optimism about the human being's ability to reach truth and certitude in moral matters, led to a strong emphasis on the power of *reason.* (Here, the word did not really mean "intelligence," but was used in the strict sense: the power of drawing valid conclusions from given premises.)

According to this older view, reason might be *aided* by faith, in the sense that faith could provide certitude in some matters where reason (after much hard labor, and by exercising a detachment which was quite rare) might reach only probable conclusions. But, according to this older view, reason did not need to be radically *healed* by faith. As a consequence of this, the attempt to fashion moral norms tended to be largely a work of reason, or philosophical thought, and the dependence of this thinking on faith consisted largely in adopting certain premises or "truths" from the Old Testament and the New Testament, and then drawing reasonable conclusions from them. But modern advances in the understanding of Scripture have not supported this approach to the Old Testament and the New, and the isolation of traditional moral theology from Scripture became more and more evident and painful.

The second factor of great significance in traditional moral thinking about norms was the preponderant role played by law. The full investigation of this question would lead us into the history of Roman law and into the study of the intriguing circumstances which led the Church to assume many of the political functions of the state after the collapse of the Western Empire—clearly issues beyond the purview of this book. However, without too much oversimplification, this could be said: from the time of the Middle Ages and almost up to the present, churchmen have viewed human existence as something essentially determined by law, and they have identified morally good activity with obedience to law. Just as civil law determined a person's relation to the state, and just as obedience to civil law marked him/her as a good citizen, so the law of God and the law of the Church (not always clearly distinguished) determined each person's relationship to that society which is called "Church," and ultimately determined each person's place in the kingdom of heaven (or outside of it).

From a very early period in the Counterreformation, Bellarmine's definition of the Church in legal terms (the "perfect society," conceived of as a kind of spiritual counterpart of earthly societies) prevailed. Up to the time of the

First Vatican Council (1870), the absolutist state provided practically the only model, and therefore it is not surprising that there was great emphasis on authority. Norms, when not evident to one and all, were simply decreed by churchmen. Furthermore, when they were so decreed, they were not regarded as factors to be weighed in the formation of one's conscience, but rather as laws to be obeyed.

There were and are many difficulties with this approach, but three should be singled out because of the harm they have done. First, this approach does not lead to responsible moral conduct, but leaves people in a state of moral adolescence or infancy, where, like children, their task is simply to obey the instructions of those who know better. Second, this emphasis on law distorts Christian existence, by making it into a life of conformity to law, rather than the fulfillment of a vocation. Third, it encourages minimalism—the zealous pursuit of those ways of fulfilling the law which entail the least possible effort and discomfort—and this leads to the development of a complicated casuistry (a body of case law and the techniques for applying it) which strips Christian existence of its personal dimension.

From about the sixteenth century up to the Second Vatican Council, moral theology was characterized, in the main, by this unhistorical approach and by this strong emphasis on law. What was called "natural law" was the central concept of moral reflection during this period, although it is important to note that the concept in use at the time was very different from the one which had been elaborated by Thomas Aquinas. The concept in use after the sixteenth century had developed in some dependence on his thought, but it was far more dependent on two other sources: on the canonical tradition of the papal court and of the faculties of law at the Italian universities, and on early modern speculation about the possibility of international law. Moral theology during this period was very confident about moral norms, and if we are to understand in what direction reflection on these problems is moving today (and perhaps in what direction it should be moving), we need to understand where it has come from.

The heart of this traditional position is this: there is an over-all norm for moral activity, and it contains within itself practical norms for all areas of human life. This norm is *human nature,* which here means "the human being considered in his/her concrete reality, and endowed with many faculties and functions, each of which has its own purpose—a purpose which was given by God, and which we know with certainty from observation and analysis."

Human nature, understood in this way, is *law,* because it is the order, the disposition, established by God in creating us, and we must respect this order if we want to act rightly. In this respect, moral theologians viewed God precisely as a lawmaker who demands obedience from his creatures. Human nature was regarded very much as the sum total of our various faculties, each of which was viewed in relative isolation from the others. Particularly in questions of medical ethics and sexual morality, it was common to examine these functions and faculties in physical and biological terms, without reference to those factors which are distinctively human (on the grounds that, whatever *additional* purposes our biological nature might serve, none of them could be allowed to violate or frustrate the physical or biological purposes themselves).

Moralists felt that natural law, in this sense, was needed for three reasons. First, they assumed that *some* law was needed for moral activity, because they could not imagine that a good moral act could be anything but an act of obedience to law. Second, Scripture (particularly the New Testament) did not contain the laws which apparently were needed to support Church teaching on a great variety of matters: private property, the proper use of sexuality, the obligation to tell the truth, Mass attendance on Sunday, the right of self-defense, and many others. Third, civil laws are not necessarily good laws, and some means must be found to distinguish good laws from bad ones. (In this matter, theologians were correct in seeing that a law is not necessarily a good law simply because it has been legislated; but they assumed, incorrectly, that a law could be judged to be bad only if it were compared with another law.)

It was common, in this older tradition, to assert that human nature (identified with natural law) *forbids* certain actions because they run counter to the purpose of one of our faculties or functions. Killing, lying, abortion, sterilization, were, in one form or another, identified as *intrinsically, objectively wrong*, and I believe that this was one of the most serious weaknesses of Christian (and, here, particularly Catholic) thinking about moral norms until the quite recent past. As we have pointed out repeatedly, external actions in themselves cannot be *morally* bad or wrong, nor can they be morally good or right; they do not merit either qualification. External actions are not in themselves moral, and they influence morality only to the extent to which they influence our decisions (which means, of course, that their influence is very great).

In the older moral tradition, decision-making became largely a process of applying general principles to specific cases. The general principle would assert that certain kinds of actions were wrong, morally evil, and then the only remaining question was: "Does this specific case fall under the general rule?" When, as often happened, this resulted in conclusions which did not seem "right," did not make sense, methods were found to temper the absoluteness of the principles. For example, not *all* killing was forbidden, but only the killing of the innocent. Abortion might be wrong in itself, but if it were the unintended by-product of another operation which could be justified on other grounds (e.g., hysterectomy in the case of uterine cancer), then it might be permitted, because in such a case it would not be *intended in itself*.

In recent years, the thinking of moral theologians has begun to change, largely because of developments in the history of thought which touched every aspect of the older view. The development of historical criticism in Germany during the course of the nineteenth century was undoubtedly the most important cause of the change, and on this question I agree fully with the evaluation of Bernard Lonergan, the Canadian Jesuit: "While elements of modern scholarship may be found here and there down through the ages, its massive development was the work of the German historical school of the nineteenth century. . . . Long resisted in Catholic circles, today it is offered no serious opposition. The era dominated by scholasticism has ended. Catholic theology is being restructured" (*Method in Theology,* 281). Lonergan's judgment is all the more remarkable because it was made by one who was well trained in scholastic philosophy and theology, and who was one of the most able practitioners of all that is of value in scholastic method.

Almost every feature of traditional moral reflection has been altered by the advance of historical-critical scholarship and by the triumph of what might be called "the historical view of the world." Human nature is no longer viewed as constant, stable, and unchangeable. We are less confident of our ability to reach the truth in many matters, and less certain of the conclusions we have drawn; and we are more aware of the fragmentary character of our knowledge.

Most important of all, historical criticism has led to a new understanding of Scripture, and to a deeper grasp, both of the nature of Jesus' call which is found in the New Testament, and of the nature of the response to that call, which is faith. As a result, there has been widespread dissatisfaction with any form of moral theology in which faith plays only a peripheral or external role. Furthermore, critical study of the New Testament has led to the insight that law and Gospel stand in an antithetical relation to each other, and has led to the demand that Christian ethics be restructured on the basis of the Gospel and not on the basis of law. But perhaps as much as any other factor, there was a growing feeling in many circles that the traditional moral theology simply "did not work"—it had an aura of the unreal about it, and people who had experimental knowledge of the areas which it addressed so confidently began in increasing numbers, to regard this traditional moral theology as simply unreal.

In the years since the Second Vatican Council (which concluded in 1965), some have confused the outmoded features which characterized some moral thought from the sixteenth century until the recent past with the great scholastic tradition, represented at its best by Thomas Aquinas. This is a mistake, not only because it is based on a serious misinterpretation of Thomas Aquinas' thought, but because any system of moral reflection which tries to dispense with his insights is rejecting something of great value. Without "natural law" in *Thomas'* sense of the word, the human task is simply incapable of fulfillment.

3.42 A Modern Statement of Thomas Aquinas' Approach

It will be useful to think of "natural law" as implying and including three insights, which can be stated quite simply. The first is the insight that human existence as a whole has a purpose, and that all of the faculties, powers, and functions which are part of human existence have their own purposes, subordinate to the overall purpose of life. (It is not at all necessary to suppose that these purposes were fixed immutably at the moment of creation. It is perfectly possible, at least within the framework of Thomas' approach to the "natural law," that a number of the purposes and finalities in human life may have evolved in the course of human cultural development.) Implied in this first insight is the conviction that there are ways of acting which lead to the fulfillment of the purposes of human existence (the overall purpose and the subordinate purposes) and that there are other ways of acting which frustrate the attainment of these purposes.

The second insight which is included in the concept of "natural law" is this: human intelligence can discover these various purposes and finalities of human life, and can discover which ways of acting are conducive to the fulfillment of those purposes, and which ways of acting will frustrate the attainment of those purposes. The third insight included in the concept of "natural law" is that it is the task of human intelligence to devise ways to promote the attainment of the over-all purpose of human life and of its subordinate purposes, and that it must do this because it is called to respect the purposiveness of human life.

It is precisely this power to discover the finality inherent in human life, and to devise ways of promoting it, which could be called "natural law." And it is for this reason that

Thomas speaks of "natural law" as the human being's participation in divine providence. Divine providence is the work of God's intelligence, as he leads creation to its appointed ends and goals. And human intelligence acts in a similar way when it perceives those ends and devises methods to insure the attainment of those goals.

What this means, of course, is that "natural law" is seriously misunderstood if it is seen as a list of arbitrary "do's" and "don'ts" inscribed on eternal tablets before the world began. Thomas Aquinas' view was very different. He gave a remarkable definition of natural law: natural law is human intelligence, precisely insofar as it can and does discern the purposes and the purposiveness of things. Without stretching Thomas' thought at all, we might summarize his view of natural law by stating the most fundamental moral principle of all: *Do all that is reasonably in your power to discover the purposes which God has for human life and for everything connected with it, and devise ways of respecting those purposes.*

Thomas' emphasis on the role of our God-given intelligence is supremely practical, and in the next chapter we will see, in outline form, how it might be applied to some practical moral questions of the day. But there is something surprising about his view: it seems to be a very "secular" (not particularly "religious") way of defining the human moral task, and in fact it is precisely that. This suggests in turn that the role of Christian faith in our moral lives is to make it possible for us to use our intelligence in the way in which it should be used (and this is a theme we will examine in Chapter 7). Thomas' practical approach will help us make another very important distinction: the question of whether a given way of acting is objectively unworthy of being chosen is *not* the same as the question of which means will be appropriate and effective in preventing such actions. This distinction will help us choose practical and effective means to help people see which ways of acting are unworthy of being chosen, and it will make us emphasize a pragmatic approach in all things. Our task is not to master the *rhetoric* of love (or "compassion"), or to achieve a warm inner feeling because we are "on the right side," but rather to choose practical and effective ways of helping people see the truth and do it.

3.43 A New Approach to the Problem of Norms

Of course, it is not enough to simply quote Thomas Aquinas on the question of natural law today. In fact, it will be almost impossible to preserve the *substance* of Thomas' approach if we insist on holding on to his *terminology*. Furthermore, some distinctively modern questions and problems have arisen in connection with the growth in autonomy of the human subject—a development which Thomas could hardly have foreseen.

As we have seen, the "solution" offered by situation ethics to the problem of the subjective element in the moral decision is little better than trendy psychobabble (or that even more repulsive subspecies: theobabble). On the other hand, our brief comments on the tradition in moral theology in the centuries after Thomas indicated that there were some serious problems with this tradition, and that many of its assumptions should be questioned. We need to conserve the positive values of that tradition, but we have to be more careful about the use of words, and more realistic about the possibilities for certitude which life offers.

Our approach will try to identify the *objective* element in moral norms. Norms are based on the realities of life, in us, in others, and in the world at large. The world is *there*, independently of our likes and dislikes, and it makes demands on us, whether we approve or not. But at the same time, we need an approach to norms which recognizes that *only decisions* can be *morally* good or bad, and that it is the *relation* of the decision to an objective situation which determines whether the decision is morally good or morally bad, right or wrong.

If this approach is to succeed, we will have to find the answer to three questions: *First,* what is the objectively real element outside of us which has this special relationship to our decisions? *Second,* what is the subjective element in the decision-making process? *Third,* what is the relation of the objective and subjective elements to each other and to the whole process?

3.44 The Objective Element in Moral Norms

Until well into this century, moral theologians argued that the objectively real element which we must recognize in decision-making is the *objective moral norm,* and this expression was taken to mean "a standard of human activity which we must acknowledge and accept." As we have noted above, this "objective moral norm" was often identified with the natural law, and many moral theologians spoke as though the essential moral task consisted in two things: first, in accepting the validity of the natural law, and, second, in determining under which "paragraph" of the natural law the case under discussion fell.

This approach represented a serious misunderstanding of our responsibility, and it was based on an inadequate theory of knowledge. A norm or standard of morality is always a *statement* which judges certain ways of acting as worthy of being chosen and others as not worthy of being chosen. Because norms are judgments, they are mental acts, acts of human imagination and intelligence, and they reside in the minds of those who make them. If many people happen to make similar judgments, then in this looser sense we can speak of the "norms of the group" or the "norms of society"—always with the understanding that the "group" or "society" as such cannot make a judgment; only its individual members can.

The objective element in our decision-making—the element which we are called to acknowledge—is not a norm. It is rather a quality which human action possesses, which is based on the relationship of a given action or way of acting to the over-all purpose of human existence and to the subordinate purposes which help to attain that over-all purpose. This quality could be called "suitability for attaining its purpose," or "essential creativity"—the word "essential" shows that the creativity belongs to the way of acting *in itself,* independently of our likes and dislikes, and the word "creativity" refers to the productiveness, the effectiveness of these ways of acting in promoting the attainment of the goal of human existence. Some ways of acting are, in themselves, creative, because they lead to the attainment of the human goal. Other ways of acting are destructive because they lead away from it. The individual actions in question could be called "creative" or "destructive ways of acting": the creative patterns or structures of our actions can be called *values.*

These "values," these "valuable" ways of acting, do not inhabit some abstract Platonic world of pure ideas or forms; they are embodied in the real situations which we meet in the real world; they are implied by the human condition and they are a part of it. But they do not depend on us as individuals. We depend on them, and if we fail to acknowledge them, we do it at the risk of losing our humanity.

We can think of these values, these essentially creative (and these anti-values, or destructive) "ways of acting" as *patterns* or *styles* of action, which either already exist or which we can bring about in the future. As human beings, we have the power to observe patterns of action and to note that many of the elements are *repeatable*—very similar actions could be performed in other circumstances. We can think about these similar ways of acting and strive to bring about situations in which they become real, and it is in this thought and planning, these attempts to devise and implement essentially creative ways of acting, that the human moral task is fulfilled. These patterns, these *moral values* are not abstract and impersonal laws which clash with the uniqueness of the individual situation; they are a *call* and a *summons* to create value in the uniqueness of the moment.

Remember that the question of whether or not people are *aware* of the essential creativity of certain ways of acting and of the essential destructiveness of others *has nothing whatsoever* to do with the question of whether these ways of acting *are* creative or destructive. It can be useful to ask why some people, or many, fail to see that ways of acting have these qualities, and it is important to point out that, at times and through no fault of their own, some people may not be responsible for the harm which they do. But the creativity and destructiveness which ways of acting possess are an objectively real part of the human situation, and they do not depend for their existence on being known and acknowledged either by individuals or by society as a whole.

3.45 The Subjective Element in Moral Norms

Although creative and destructive actions are objectively real, and although the patterns and structures of such actions (what I have called "values") are objective in the sense that they are *there*, whether or not we choose to recognize them, moral norms, as we have seen, have a somewhat different status. Norms are *subjective* in the proper sense of the word: they are acts of a human *subject*. ("Subjective" should not be used in the sense of "depending entirely on the individual, relative, simply a matter of feeling"; this is a very inaccurate use of the word.) Like all acts of the human subject, they are acts of knowledge and will, acts of knowing and loving, and they are real, precisely in this sense. Our subjective acts of knowing and loving (or of refusing to know and of hating) are some of the most real things in our lives, and they are the cause of all of the changes we bring about in our world. We must, of course, raise the question of whether our acts of knowing do justice to the real world, whether they are judgments which respect the way things really *are*. If they do not, then we need some way to refer to that fact, but to call them "subjective" in such cases really misses the point. In the proper sense, all judgments are subjective.

It is obvious that no two human beings, no two subjects, ever find themselves in *exactly* the same situation, but the judgments which we are called upon to make about these situations will be either true or false, and this truth or falsity is determined by whether or not our judgments reflect the reality of the situation and of the demands which it makes upon us. The question is not whether or not a judgment is subjective—*all* judgments are. The real question is that of whether or not the judgment is valid and correct because it is a true statement (by this human subject) about the way things *really are*.

3.46 The Relationship of the Subjective and Objective Elements in Decision-Making

It would be tempting to say that our basic human obligation is to choose values, valuable ways of acting, and to avoid ways of acting which compromise or destroy those values, but this would be an oversimplification. Much of the time it seems very difficult to discover just what and where the values are. Even more frequently, the same action which will be creative from one point of view will be destructive from another, so that decision-making is rarely a simple process of choosing creativity over destructiveness. What makes our decisions morally good is the *truly serious intent* to discover those ways of acting which are creative, more creative, less destructive.

Does this mean that, in the final analysis, the demands of the objectively real situation are not important and only our intentions count? By no means. What it means is that *the only intention* which can be called morally right and good is the intention to discover those ways of acting which are essentially creative or destructive, *in themselves and quite independently of us.* This intention is the basic decision in which the human being rejects radical selfishness and renounces the claim to be the center of the universe, around which all else revolves. The serious attempt to discover creative ways of acting, to discover real values, is the serious intent to discover who I really am as I stand in the presence of God, and in a world with other human beings. It is the decision to take every practical step to dispel darkness, uncertainty, and doubt about the values in life and about their relative importance. It is the decision to make these values normative for myself.

The intent to discover real value obviously includes the conviction that real value is there to be discovered, and it includes the conviction that when we discover it, we find something which transcends us, individually and collectively, and which therefore makes unconditional claims on us. It seems clear that this intent and this knowledge are, at least implicitly, the recognition of the reality of God. To respect reality and its mystery, to admire its charm and its beauty, to let ourselves be claimed by it and to willingly respond to it, is implicitly to know and love the infinite One on whom we depend totally.

Note, however, that there may be practical reasons why many people who intend to act rightly and well do not "believe in God"—that is, do not accept the existence, the reality, of that which they *think* the word "God" means. For such people, the existence of values which transcend us and which claim us can function as a *pseudonym* under which the real God appears (and perhaps this is the only way in which the real God can appear at certain times in history). For such people, the committed search for value and the desire to make such value, once discovered, normative in life is the form taken by faith, and possesses the basic structure of the act of faith. In this sense, I believe that it is true to say that without faith in God there can be no morally good commitment or morally good choices. But the faith in God of which we are speaking here is often far from explicit, and in such cases we might aptly speak of anonymous believers.

The distinction between values and norms is particularly useful because it emphasizes an important fact: the proper stance of the human being toward moral norms is *not* that of obediently accepting a moral standard which is already there; it is rather the difficult and lifelong task of learning to recognize values, of estimating their relative importance and the seriousness of the demands which they make upon us, and of learning from our successes and failures as we try to implement and realize them. Moral norms are not lists of arbitrary "do's" and "don'ts" to which we must conform. Rather, they are *deliberately intelligent judgments* about styles and patterns of activity which foster or frustrate the attainment of our purpose as human beings.

They are the expression of our free commitment to discover the truth so that we may do it, and it is this which accounts for the moral goodness of the decision to create moral norms for ourselves.

The moral task is not precisely that of making judgments which are objectively correct—no one can guarantee that. The real moral task is that of *doing all that is reasonably in our power to make such judgments.* It is never enough to "do what we feel is right" if this means to "let the situation 'speak' to us and then to act on the basis of a 'gut feeling.' " Doing what we feel is right is a guarantee of acting rightly only when we have done all that is reasonably in our power to make sure that the decision which we feel is right is *really right,* because it is a decision in favor of a value which is *really there.*

3.47 Some Important Conclusions

First: We are Responsible for Good Moral Norms.

This suggests that it is above all in the very process of *fashioning* our moral norms that we act rightly or wrongly, because it is here that our commitment in favor of or against intelligent ways of acting will be manifest. Moral norms are not simply "there" for us to accept or reject; we are *responsible* for fashioning good ones. The real question for Christian ethics and moral theology is not that of how to discover pre-existent moral norms, but is rather the question of how to make deliberately intelligent judgments about the kinds of actions which foster or frustrate the attainment of the human goal—that is, it is the question of how to *fashion* moral norms.

Second: Our Normative Judgments Must Reflect Values Which Are Objectively There.

The task of making deliberately intelligent judgments

in moral matters is difficult and complex, and both of these factors might lead to discouragement and even despair. However, there is a simple insight which can be the source of confidence and hope. It points to a matter of great moral significance which is also the only valid reason for trying to make good moral judgments in any area. The simple insight is this: in every concrete and unique situation in which we find ourselves, there *are* objective values which stand in a real relation of relative importance and which therefore make real and objective demands on us. The judgments which we make about such situations will be either true or false (and can be so in varying degrees) and their truth or falsity depends on whether or not they do justice to the objective situation.

3.48 The Tension between Norm and Context in Christian Ethics

If we are clear about this insight, then there is no difficulty in admitting that the views of society, the opinions of men and women of good will, the limitations imposed by the historical epoch in which we live, all play a very important role in decision-making. But these various conditioning factors *do not* determine whether ways of acting in themselves are valuable or not. They have no effect whatsoever on the reality of value and its presence in a concrete situation. What they do affect (and often limit) is our *ability to perceive* the values which are there. We are to a great extent dependent on others for our perception of value (to a degree greater than we care to admit), and if others have failed in their responsibility to us, we may make errors in judgment about value, for which we bear little or no responsibility. (And, of course, we may bear much of the responsibility for the erroneous judgments of others if we have failed in our responsibility to them.) In the same way, we are affected by the *mores,* the habitual moral judgments, which are current in an entire civilization and culture. Often these judgments carry such a weight of numbers and of history that it is difficult for the individual to prevail against them. This does not mean that it is a morally good or even tolerable thing for an individual to simply accept the bad moral judgments of a majority; it does mean that under the pervasive influence of moral judgments held by almost all of those whom we know and respect, it can be extremely difficult to make correct judgments about the objective values which are really or potentially present in a concrete situation.

The conviction of the objectivity of moral value is the only basis on which a meaningful ethical system can be built. In the absence of this conviction, we human beings become warped parodies of ourselves, and all talk of acting rightly or wrongly becomes an exercise in futility. It is quite true that there is something unique about every situation in which we are called to make a decision, and it is true that these situations cannot be typed or classified so accurately that decision-making could be reduced to the application of general norms or rules of conduct to specific cases. No ethical system should ever deny this. But there is an objective element in every unique situation, and it consists in the fact that the values, personal and material, about which we are called to decide *are objectively real,* and stand in a network of relationships which are *there,* whether we like it or not. And no ethical system should ever deny this either.

If we are clear about this fact, then we can afford to be frank about the difficulties which we almost always encounter when we try to discover these values, and we can be tolerant of the failure of ourselves and others to discover these values and to implement them. But at the same time we can approach these failures with confidence, and with the conviction that it is worth trying again to discover these elusive values.

3.5 NATURAL LAW AND THE PROBLEM OF DISAGREEMENT ABOUT THE GOALS AND PURPOSES OF LIFE

It is true that when people are asked to specify the end and goal of human existence in terms of *content,* and to describe it in some concrete detail, there will be as many answers as people polled. However, although their answers differ widely in respect to *content,* there is something about the *attitude* they have toward their differing views which is very interesting. Although the *content* of their views is quite different, their *attitude* toward the content is almost identical. In all cases, those who argue in favor of their own views of the purpose of human existence (even in the "non-argumentative" sense of holding it themselves) *claim to have found the truth and to be worth listening to for precisely that reason.* They claim to be talking sense and not nonsense. They claim to have found a truth about the human situation which is valid not only for themselves but for others as well (in the sense that it would be good if others adopted their views, at least to the extent of leaving them alone and not trying to change them). The fact that they write books, teach classes, and in various ways engage in propaganda for their views is cogent evidence of this.

These facts suggest that it might be possible to specify the purpose of human existence, not immediately in terms of *content,* but in terms of the *intent* which is evident when people begin to speak about their idea of the end or goal of life. If human beings are always trying to reach the truth about the human condition, and if they claim truth for the views they have arrived at, and argue that all should act in accordance with the truth which they have found, then it would appear that *there is one thing for which we are called to strive simply because we are human: we strive to know the truth about ourselves so that we may do it.* It is distinctively and in-alienably human to reach for the truth, to try to under-stand oneself and one's world, to discern objective values and to urge them on others precisely because they are ob-jective. This is a most interesting facet of our nature, and it is one which needs no additional proof, because it has the most powerful of all proofs behind it: it cannot be coher-ently denied, *because the denial itself would be the claim to have found the truth and to see in that truth a value which should be communicated to others.*

3.51 The Purpose of Human Life: A Second Look

Now it might appear that we have not gained a great deal in making this point. To talk about the purpose of hu-man life as "knowing the truth and doing it" seems vague and nebulous in the face of almost universal disagreement about what the truth consists in. However, specifying the human goal in terms of *intent* has some important impli-cations in terms of *content*. Three of the most important are worth noting.

First, as human beings, we have to *ask* about the mean-ing of our lives and of our world. The search for meaning leads us outside of ourselves and outside of the historical moment in which we live. This is obvious, because we ask about the deepest meaning of our lives, and although we look as deeply within ourselves as we can, we try to make judgments about ourselves and our world from a vantage point which is necessarily outside and beyond both (and which must be, because it is a vantage point from which we criticize both). To be intent on knowing the truth and doing it is to admit that there *are* objective values and that they *claim us unconditionally.*

Second, we ask the question of meaning not only in regard to ourselves, as though our lives were enclosed, private areas, of significance to ourselves alone. We ask the same question about every situation, every encounter, everything which touches our lives. But again, to ask about the meaning of something is to judge it in terms of something beyond it—it is to hold it up in the light and examine it in terms of an ideal which transcends it. We quite confidently ask about the meaning of anything and everything, and this is a sign, not only that we transcend ourselves, but that we are striving to make judgments in terms of an ideal which transcends every finite thing, actual or possible.

This is the most basic fact of our existence, and it is responsible for the deepest anxiety which can afflict us. If we locate the meaning of our lives in any finite thing— money, property, power, pleasure—we abandon at that moment the search for the transcendent and the infinite and *we abandon ourselves.* And we are aware of this; we become restless and disoriented, and we are driven to amass more and more of whatever finite good we have made absolute in our lives. If this finite good is the self, then we are haunted by the realization that when this self is gone, when we die, all is lost, because we know in the depths of our being that the truth which does not transcend the self is not really truth at all.

A third implication of the principle of knowing the truth and doing it is that the ultimate end of human existence is not limited to time, but is eternal, and that consequently the human person has infinite value. In other words, the human being is never a means, only an end. (To speak of the end and goal of human existence as transcending time obviously raises the question of God again, and forces us to ask if belief in God is a condition for authentic moral commitment. As we have already noted, *implicit* belief in God is such a condition, but this belief does not *necessarily* avail itself of the word "God" or of any of the other religious trappings of ordinary belief. In fact, the conviction that human existence has an end which transcends time is another "pseudonym" of God.)

3.6 SUMMARY AND OUTLOOK

We have talked about moral norms, about the status of such norms (where they come from), about why they are needed, and about the problems they pose. It was also our purpose to suggest a general direction to be taken for solving these problems, but the accent was strongly on the word "general." On a number of occasions we mentioned the serious problem posed by the fact that human beings, even intelligent men and women of good will, do not agree, either on the over-all purpose of human life, or on the subordinate purposes of various human powers and functions and various elements which make up human life. We concluded by pointing out that the attempt to specify the goal of human life in terms of *intent* rather than content might suggest a way of dealing with the problem of the over-all goal of human life. This approach might, paradoxically, suggest that there are some elements of *content* which people share without fully realizing it, particularly in regard to some deep questions about our need for transcendence and about the fact that need appears in some way in all of our decisions.

But important as these conclusions are, they leave us

with some practical problems which cannot be avoided in any serious treatment of moral norms, and which can be grouped under three headings: First: what does the individual do when faced with the problem of conflicting values—that is, when the same action or way of acting is, at the same time (and in different respects) both worthy and unworthy of being chosen? Second: what do we do about the problem of conflicting normative judgments being made by different individuals? Who has the right to decide which ways of acting are, *in themselves,* worthy of being chosen and which are not worthy of being chosen? And third: what do we do when these differences of opinion touch, not only questions of the private conduct of individuals, but questions of the rights of others? In other words, what is the relationship between morality and law?

It is not very useful to discuss these questions in the abstract, and, in fact, reflection on them makes sense only in terms of a practical and workable system of moral norms. The following chapter is designed as an *illustration,* in skeletal form, of just such a system, and it will make it possible to deal with the three questions just enumerated, in Chapter 5.

4

A Sample System
of Ethical Values

We have seen some of the problems involved in recognizing values and in using them to create moral norms to live by. As might be suspected, the most difficult task is that of weighing values which are in competition in a given case, and of developing methods of resolving conflicts among values as perceived by different individuals. But before turning to this task, we will need to have an idea of what the competing values *are*, so that we can illustrate the process of assessing values in the concrete.

The only practical way of doing this is to present a brief moral "system" which strives to identify the fundamental values of human life and to determine why they are values. Each of the values mentioned here would really need at least a book-length essay to explain its meaning and to justify its inclusion, and therefore what is presented here should be seen as a skeleton or an outline of a system of moral norms—a system which claims to be the work of intelligent reflection and analysis. Such an outline is not an unchanging foundation which will never need to be reexamined; it is rather a proposal which can become more probable in time, as we experiment with it and find that it works. After what was said in the last chapter about the status of norms, we hardly need to point out that these norms are not "out there" in (or above) the world. They were, and are, in the mind of the writer. They are judgments proposed for examination, and the question of whether or not they are based on a knowledge of reality as it is remains an open question.

The moral judgments which we make are always the attempt to answer questions. And in fact, the morally good act of striving to make deliberately intelligent judgments about value is a matter of allowing the right questions to be raised, and of not resting until adequate answers are found. Sometimes we raise these questions explicitly, sometimes implicitly. But at times we should make all of them explicit, to make sure that we are not living the unexamined, and therefore the inhuman, life. Of course the presupposition for raising questions about value is the existence of such value. More generally, the presupposition is *the intelligibility of the world and of the human condition.* Unless the world is intelligible, unless it makes sense, the inquiry into value is not only unproductive; it is impossible.

4.1 THE VALUE ON WHICH ALL OTHERS REST

The question which reveals what can be called the *foundational* value is this: in the case at hand (that is, in whatever decision one is about to make), is the most fundamental value of all at stake—that is, the *existence,* in the real world, of values which lay claim to us simply because they are *there?* Ordinarily this value is present as a ground or basis on which other values rest, but there are times when we have to face the issue directly. Not only philosophers and theologians, but teachers and writers have the task of affirming and defending the objectivity of value, the reality and intelligibility of the human goal, and the fact that there are ways of acting which lead us toward that goal and other ways of acting which turn us away from it.

4.11 Our Basic Responsibility

Those working in the media have serious responsibilities here, as do educated people in general, and, in fact, all whose intelligence and leadership abilities give them influence over others. To take these responsibilities seriously is to speak out against the *relativizing* of value, against the claim that "it all depends on how you see it," etc. To take these responsibilities seriously is to argue honestly and persuasively in favor of those demands which the real world makes on us in virtue of our common humanity. The educational establishment has often failed in this and has frequently become the mouthpiece of an empty relativism. However, as we have pointed out above, a poorly thought out theory of objective value, together with inaccurate ways of thinking and speaking about the objective element in moral norms, must bear some of the blame. Frequently enough in the past, customs, conventions, and traditional ways of acting have been identified with objective value, while partial values and even non-values have been made into absolutes. Unfortunately the rejection of these false values and stances has led many in our day to deny the existence of any objective values at all.

One final observation is important. Although cases in which we are explicitly called on to defend the objectivity of value are relatively rare, this value is often present in disguised form. When we tire in our effort to discover the values in life, we are often tempted to excuse our laziness on the grounds that the real values simply do not exist and that it is therefore futile to waste time in trying to discover them. Faced with this situation it is good to remember that to fail and admit it is never a moral disaster; to deny the fact of failure is another matter.

4.12 Foundational Value and the Existence of God

The acceptance of the intelligibility of the world is already, as we have pointed out, a hidden but real way of knowing God, and it is an interesting and valid way of raising the question of God. In this sense the real God is the foundation of all moral commitment; the existence of God is a condition of possibility for the existence of a moral order and of the objective values on which it is based; and knowledge of the existence of God is a condition for acting in a morally good way. But this knowledge may be *implicit*—in the sense that an individual might not be aware of knowing God as a person—and perhaps this is the case more often in our day than in earlier epochs of history.

4.2 THE DIGNITY OF THE HUMAN PERSON AS THE MOST IMPORTANT CREATED VALUE

4.21 Expressing This Value in Religious and Secular Terms

The human person has unlimited, unconditioned value, and this value can be expressed in both religious and secular terms. People with a religious view of the world will think of God as the one who has loved them with an everlasting love and they will understand human existence as the response to a call which was voiced before the world began. For them, to be human is to be in dialogue with the "High and Holy One," and it is therefore to transcend the limited and the finite. For those who believe in God, eternal life is rooted in the dialogue with God, through which we are taken into the very life of God and become in that event immune to the assault of death.

This same value can be expressed in non-religious terms, and this could take the following form. We are claimed first of all by the value of truth, because from our earliest days we are gripped by the desire to know. As children we raise incessant questions, and the great achievements of natural science result from the desire to find the key to the unity and intelligibility of the natural world. We have a hunger for all that *is*, a thirst for reality, and an accompanying ability to recognize limited reality when we find it, and we assess with remarkable confidence its claims to be real. To be human is to be open to the *infinite* and therefore to recognize the *finite*, to be aware of its limitations, and to be troubled by them.

The grandeur and tragedy of the human condition spring from the same root: we yearn for infinity. We are called to a place which is beyond the created world, and in some way this transcendent reality is foreshadowed in the quest in which human intelligence is always engaged. And yet, of ourselves, we possess nothing; we must find ourselves, and our personhood is not something given to us but something to be achieved.

Whether we use religious language (and talk about ourselves as "the response to a call which was voiced before the world began") or use secular language (and talk about "human intelligence and its quest for the transcendent"), it is clear that what we are speaking of here is the ground and basis of the infinite dignity of the human person.

4.22 Self-Love as an Essential Value

If the human person has infinite dignity, then we will have to conclude that the dignity of one's own self, one's own person, is foremost among essential values, and that for this reason our first moral task is to love ourselves, and, specifically, to love that within us which constitutes us as persons in the full sense of the word: our capacity to know and love the truth. Many people find this principle shocking. If they are religious, they may feel that their faith demands that they put others first ("A man can have no greater love than to lay down his life for his friends"). And if they are not religious, they may feel that there is something selfish about self-love and that it is a sign of a self-centered life. They may, with very good reason, be more than a little disgusted with the narcissism of the human potential movement. They are probably mildly amused at the antics of their friends who are "into" transcendental meditation, transactional analysis, EST (or whatever psychological panacea comes down the pike next spring) but their amusement is often tinged with distaste for the total absorption with self which is characteristic of such movements. Most of us would still like to pay at least lip-service to the ideal of self-sacrifice.

But this tendency to see moral goodness only in actions which seek to promote the welfare of others has deeper roots. It springs from the modern tendency to see sin or wrong-doing exclusively in terms of the harm done directly to others. Statements such as these are typical and are accepted uncritically: "The only sin is the failure to love others" or "We can only do evil in violating the integrity and rights of the other person." This modern tendency itself has two apparently unrelated roots; one of them is religious (and comes in two versions), and the other is secular.

Self-love has repeatedly been censured from within the Christian tradition. For John Calvin, one of the founding fathers of the Protestant Reformation, it is man's duty to will only the glory of God, and self-love is to be avoided at all costs. Ignatius Loyola, the founder of the Jesuit order, speaks in a similar vein. The motto of his order is "Ad Majorem Dei Gloriam"—For the greater glory of God—and he speaks in his Spiritual Exercises of the need to "conquer self," "eliminate self-love," "seek to be despised and humiliated," and so on.

Much in the monastic tradition, going back as far as the desert fathers in Egypt (about the middle of the third century), seems to say the same thing. We find in this tradition repeated exhortations to mortification, which is understood not precisely in terms of self-inflicted punishment, but rather as an effective way of putting an end to self-love. This tradition itself is ostensibly based on Jesus' words in the ninth chapter of Mark's Gospel (". . . unless a man deny himself and take up his cross, he cannot be my disciple"). But the use of this text in the ascetical tradition is, to some extent, not based on good exegesis. Jesus was not an ascetic, and in the Synoptic tradition there are some traces of Christian embarrassment at this fact. For Jesus, it is clear that there is a false kind of self-love which must be rejected, but it is equally clear that there is a true kind of self-love which must be cultivated, and this is obvious if we read the rest of the text from Mark which was cited just a few lines above. The real goal is not losing one's life but gaining it; and the gaining of one's own life is Mark's idiom for what is called here "self-love."

A second reason for which Christians hesitate to see self-love as an essential value is their embarrassment at the past failures of Christianity. Up to the recent past, sin was thought of in very individualistic terms—as the action in which an individual violated the law of God—and it was judged to be bad or wrong for just that reason: it affected God and the individual, and it had little or nothing to do with the relation of the Christian to others. Complaints about "Sunday Christians" who despise their fellow human beings and define faith solely in terms of the fulfillment of ritual obligations and tabuistic law are based on real abuses. Renewed study of the Gospels has shown that Jesus had little use for ritual law, and that he insisted that one's stance toward God was manifest in one's stance toward the neighbor. From this, many Christians in our own time have drawn the invalid conclusion that one's stance toward God is *identical* to one's stance toward the neighbor, and that the only sin is the failure to love the neighbor.

Finally, modern man's reserve in regard to self-love has non-religious roots as well. We all desire the complete control of our own lives. We want to "do what we please," at least within the confines of our own lives, and we suspect (not without reason) that *true* love of self would interfere with this line of conduct. We suspect that true love of self would force us to locate and identify the values in our own lives, and then to do all in our power to promote and respect them. We suspect that true love of self would force us to admit that to choose to promote value is right and to choose not to do it is wrong. This fact shows something of great importance: our modern craving for autonomy (in the sense of being able to do just what we please) is nothing more than a *thinly disguised contempt of self*. There is a tragic split in the ego of self-styled "modern" (wo)men: they are totally dedicated to a self which they insist on stripping of all value.

It is worth noting that the widespread modern rejection of self-love and of the values of self-love has not led to selflessness. It has led rather to ethical paralysis in all areas of life, because it makes it impossible to take any values seriously, and *for this reason it makes both love of God and love of neighbor impossible.* We are called on as human beings to see reality and truth as values, and we are called on to love life. And the very first part of reality which we are called on to value and love is that part of it which is given to us: our own lives. Our dedication to truth and reality is measured by our dedication to that part of reality which God has given to us. The real world and all those in it lay claim to us and ask us to respect and promote their integrity, their wholeness, and their harmony, and they ask us to do all in our power to insure that they remain whole and unscarred. But our lives are our *share in the world,* and in those who are part of that world.

A few simple questions can show why we cannot love either God or our neighbor unless we love ourselves. How can the other person, the neighbor, be of value, if I am not? What is this mysterious quality which he/she possesses which is lacking in me? If I am without value, how could it possibly be a good thing for me to love another? Unless I am of very great value, then when I love my neighbor I give to him or her nothing of value. How can I love God if I despise what he has given to me? But his greatest gift to me is my own life, my own self, my own personhood. Finally, Paul asks an interesting question in the eighth chapter of his letter to the Romans: "If God is for us, who is against us?" If God is *for* us, how can we refuse to be *for ourselves?*

All of these questions show that we can recognize the dignity and worth of others only if we recognize our own dignity and worth. Christian faith does not call on us to love others and despise ourselves, but rather to love others *as we love ourselves.* Our neighbor is not in competition with us for our love; we have selves worth giving only if we have selves worth loving. (In the next chapter we will point out that authentic love of self is something very difficult to attain, and that in point of fact it can be attained only in dialogue with God, but this will not call into question any of the points made here.)

4.23 Our Words, Ourselves

Our human dignity is very much at stake in the words we speak, and a brief reflection on honesty and integrity in this respect will deepen our understanding of authentic self-love. We are those to whom God speaks and we are those who can turn back to God in gratitude and speak to him. We are those who discover ourselves in the accepting and loving word of another, and we are those who confer real existence on others when we speak the right word to them. Speech is not merely an action we engage in and from which we could distance ourselves. Our words are an extension and prolongation of our very selves: we are in them, and they carry our personal reality into those situations in which we speak. In our words we commit *ourselves* or we refuse that commitment, and it is for this reason that *honesty* is so high a human value. And it is also for this reason that the basic question we should ask when we try to make a decision which respects the essential values of our lives is this: Does this decision touch the integrity and honesty of my own self? Does it touch the inner unity and consistency of my person? Does this decision involve the implicit truthfulness of my word, which is the truthfulness of my very self?

Each of these questions is a way of expressing the inalienable dignity of the human person, which is rooted in the fact that a person is never a means to an end but only and always an end or goal in him/herself. We have to ask one question as we confront every moral decision: Are we toying with a choice which will, perhaps in a very subtle way, compromise our ability to perceive the truth and our ability to act in freedom, and are we *using* ourselves to gain money, property, and the esteem of others, or to prevent the loss of these things?

Codes of chivalry, and, in more recent times, codes of honor, attempted to safeguard this value. As was almost inevitable, they did it in a rather conventional way, confusing honor with certain rules of conduct which were recognized by society or by some group or class within society. There has always been a measure of hypocrisy in such matters, but on the positive side these codes of honor made people aware that there were certain values which were worthy of our attention and that it was shameful to despise them. The crisis of the "honor system" in military academies is a good example of the ambiguity of these codes. If they are seen as nothing more than the ground rules of a moribund military caste system, they will have no power to motivate conduct. But, ideally, these codes of honor point to some of the fundamental values of life, because they affirm that the real man/woman is one who, without coercion, will stamp certain ways of acting as a threat to his/her inner unity, consistency, wholeness, and truth.

To some degree, these codes and the ethic they were designed to enforce have declined with the demise of the Protestant ethic in the United States. This ethical system was stern in condemning any lapses of duty, and viewed them as personal sins which would be judged with severity by an all-seeing God, who was thought of as a somber chairman of the board. Obviously, even when this ethic was in full vigor, honorable men/women were a rarity, but the ideal was recognized as an ideal, and it was operative on many levels of society.

4.24 The Significance of Honesty and Honor in the Contemporary Moral Discussion

Many people today are critical of the breakdown of morality in political and economic life, but the critics are not too sure of what is wrong, and they tend to speak in rather vague terms of "respect for the rights of others," or of "protection from undue interference," or of "the right to do what one pleases, as long as no one is hurt." But there is no evidence that vague values like these (at *best* they are partial and derived) have any power to motivate the individual to act in a morally good way.

Here, too, we have to distinguish concern for morality in public life from mastery of the *rhetoric* of concern. It is obvious that in our day we need a firm and well-reasoned reassertion of the objectivity of value, but much of the hand-wringing that has been going on since the late sixties and early seventies illustrates not the concern for moral values but rather the capacity for sustained hypocrisy which is a rather unattractive feature of the American character, and which is probably a legacy of New England Puritanism.

What we do need is a strong statement that the dignity, the integrity, and the inviolability of the human person (starting with that person for whom we ourselves bear the greatest responsibility—the self) are among the highest of the universal moral values which claim us. We must learn to ask, and we must teach others to ask, this question: Is the honorable man/woman a naive fool who refuses to face reality, or is he/she right in holding to a kind of integrity, in the absence of which human life is a parody and a hollow pretense? This is the question which we should ask insistently in the worlds of business and politics, and techniques for raising it should be discussed at all stages of the educational process.

We have to learn that in matters of social or public morality, there is no relevance whatsoever to the question of whether, for example, the insurance company or the federal government will suffer serious losses because of our dishonesty. The real question is not that of which partner can more gracefully absorb the loss; something much deeper is at stake, and something with much more dangerous implications. The real question is whether in acting dishonestly we are creating models of action which will destroy us, insidiously but surely.

An example will be useful here: it is often argued that it is wrong for public or corporate officials to take a bribe, because it is the taking of money to which the official has no right. But if this were the only consideration, the individual taking the bribe might easily argue that he/she is underpaid, and that no social or individual harm will come from accepting the bribe (and this seems to be the process of reasoning which is used by most bribees). However, the real point at issue is this: one who takes a bribe indicates that he/she can be bought, and that his/her word cannot be relied on. The same is true of cheating in school or in business, or of defrauding the government or a large corporation of either money or goods. In each case we are dealing with a form of lying: as public or corporate officials, we have made an implied promise to make decisions on the basis of objective evidence, and we have gone back on our word.

Honesty, of course, does not demand naiveté. Honesty and integrity are values, but the concrete form which they take depends very much on the individual situation and on the ground rules of that situation which are (or should be) known by all of the participants. Honesty and integrity do not force a defense lawyer who knows that his client is guilty to admit that fact in public. The integrity of the lawyer demands precisely the opposite, because the task of the defense lawyer is to use all of his skill and all of the resources of the law in an adversary situation, and to serve justice by doing precisely that. If the legislator (and, in a democracy, ultimately the people) believe that there are too many loopholes in the law and that the guilty are going unpunished, then it is *their* task to change the law. It is never the task of the defense lawyer to do less than his best. These ground rules of legal procedure are clear and the principals in any courtroom drama agree on them, but the general public is surprisingly ignorant of these facts. (Obviously, if a lawyer tells his client to lie under oath or if he bribes witnesses, he compromises his integrity, and, in addition, he inflicts serious harm on the legal system.)

In these areas many cases of conflict can arise—cases in which honesty and integrity seem to be compromised by either of the choices one might make. Here, two comments are in order. First, such cases should be examined to make sure that the conflict is real. If it is, then it is often worth asking if some change in the situation or some clarification would remove the conflict. If this is the case, obviously these steps should be taken. Second, if honest examination reveals that the conflict is real and that nothing can be done about it, then clearly the choice should fall on that course of action which involves the least loss of integrity. (In a later section we will develop techniques to deal with this type of problem.)

Some cases of apparent conflict arise because of another fact. There are "shadowy" areas in life, where ways of acting which appear to be somewhat dishonest have become "institutionalized"—that is, they are understood and accepted by all of the participants. Certain parts of the federal and state income tax forms probably belong here: if one itemizes, it is assumed that there is a certain "fair" or expected percentage of gross income which will be taken under the heading of charitable deductions, or as costs of entertaining clients and the like. In such cases, where there is a common understanding, assumed and accepted, at least tacitly, by all of the participants, the integrity of the individual is ordinarily not compromised when he/she acts in accord with this understanding.

But this situation is not without danger, because it is easy to slip into another kind of "justification": "everybody does it, and therefore it must be morally acceptable." In such situations we ought to ask whether such "understandings," such commonly acknowledged ground rules, should not be eliminated precisely because of this lack of clarity. In the long run, the expense-account lunch can lead to personal dishonesty and to contempt for law in much the same way as that in which the modest Christmas gift offered to members of the local police department can compromise equitable law enforcement. The principles seem clear enough in such matters, but practices need to be developed by those in these different professions, and they should be stated clearly both for those within each profession and for those outside.

At the end of this digression we can summarize these reflections on self-love very simply: when faced with serious moral choices, the first question which each of us must ask is this: What effect will this action have on me as a *person*? Is this action beneath me because it poses a threat to my dignity and integrity as a person? There are three types or classes of actions which pose a real threat to the self and which real self-love will urge us to avoid.

4.25 Untruthfulness

Actions which are in the broadest sense *untruthful* pose a threat to our honesty and integrity, because they create a split between what we are and what we claim to be. Actions such as lying and cheating, business fraud, obsequious or fawning behavior, and all forms of disloyalty to those values which we claim to respect—all of these create an emptiness and incoherence at the center of our lives. It is true that actions of this type often infringe on the rights of others, but they are, first and foremost, actions which are destructive of ourselves, because through them we lose that wholeness and unmarred integrity which is proper to us as human beings.

4.26 Lack of Respect for the Body

In the second place among actions which pose a real threat to the self, we find those actions which harm us by damaging or destroying our power to respond to the demands of life intelligently and freely. To be a self is to be one who is capable of knowledge and love, and for the human being this means to be a *spiritual animal*—one who knows and loves as an incarnate spirit. Human knowledge and love are not only spiritual activities: they are also bodily and material activities. Love of self demands that we do nothing to destroy or compromise the bodily and material substratum of our spiritual existence, and it demands that we take reasonable care of our bodies and our health. The misuse of alcohol and drugs, massive overeating and overdrinking, come under this heading: they cripple our intelligence and they paralyze our freedom. In the sphere of sexuality, the "gourmet" and "spectator sport" aberrations come under this heading, because *they make real sexual love an impossibility,* and in so doing they destroy a very high value.

4.27 The Enslavement to Objects

In the third place we find actions which lower us to the level of mere things or objects. Here belong all of the many ways in which we *define* ourselves in terms of things: attributing ultimate value to money, possessions, property, jobs, "success," power, influence, and so on. If we are willing to define ourselves in terms of things, we quickly become nothing more or better than these things or objects themselves.

4.3 THE "OTHER", THE NEIGHBOR, AS VALUE

Personal integrity is the first among the essential values of life, and because it is an essential value, we are called to make it normative in our lives. When we do so, it directs us to see everything in life in terms of its power to promote or to impede the development of the true self—which is, of course, the self in dialogue with God.

What prevents this stance from being selfish or self-centered (in the negative sense of the word) is the phrase "true self, self in dialogue with God." The true vocation of the person is to *be there for the other,* and thus to live out the truth that we possess ourselves only when we put our existence on the line for others. Genuine human existence is existence *with* others and *for* them. We are authentic selves to the degree to which we find in the integrity of others the same kind of value (and ultimately the same value) as that which we find in our own integrity. Therefore, the *second* major question which we have to ask about essential values is this: How can the personal integrity of others (particularly of those others for whom we are especially responsible) be promoted in all that we do? Like myself, the neighbor is a person, and therefore an end or goal in him/herself and never a means. Persons are to be loved and not used.

The task of "being there for" the neighbor is best understood by reflecting on the valid claims or *titles* to certain things or to certain ways of being treated—titles which we have because of their relationship to the attainment of human dignity and integrity. These titles or valid claims are the basis of the obligations which we have to each other, and real love of the neighbor is first and foremost the willingness to take these obligations seriously. The reflection which is found in the following sections is really a reflection on the personal and social values of human life, and it will also lead to a clearer view of the values to be safeguarded in self-love.

In the sections which follow, no attempt is made to develop a set of normative principles which could apply to every case. Rather, we will try to develop, at least in general terms, the *questions* which we have to take seriously if we are going to make *deliberately intelligent judgments* about the fulfillment of our human task. To take these questions seriously is to be attentive, intelligent, reasonable, and responsible; it is to fulfill the basic moral imperative of asking what the real values in life are and how they can be intelligently safeguarded.

4.31 Freedom from Arbitrary Violence

The right to physical life itself is fundamental, because it is the basis of all other rights. Human beings have the right to a life which is not threatened by arbitrary violence on the part of others. This right is the basis of the right to self-defense; such self-defense must always be proportioned to the violence threatened, but in the view of most moral theologians it can extend to the killing of the one who threatens criminal violence, either individually or as part of a terrorist conspiracy. The right to defend oneself against arbitrary violence on the part of others includes the right to self-defense against such violence on the part of one's own government, and can include, under certain circumstances, the right to revolt. Other individuals against whom this right can be asserted are, for example, those who insist on driving while under the influence of liquor or drugs. These people threaten a fundamental human right, and we all have the right to take appropriate action against such threats. (Such appropriate action will usually consist in taking steps to keep such people off the road by imposing sanctions severe enough to dissuade them.)

The majority of moral theologians agree that innocent human life should be defended against those who would take it in order to solve some other problem, even a serious one (although there is some disagreement about whether *any* problem could be serious enough to justify it). This is the ground for opposing abortion, and the argument is based on the fact that human life, even in its earliest stages, has a dignity which does not allow us to use it as a mere means to solve problems posed by, for example, rape, or incest, or teenage pregnancy. These problems are extremely serious and they are often tragic, but even tragic problems are not appropriately solved by the taking of innocent human life (innocent, that is, in the sense that there can be no question of the voluntary forfeiture of the right to life through *one's own* criminal activity).

The same argument is valid against euthanasia: human life, even when weak and fragile, has a dignity which will not tolerate the decision of others to terminate it on the grounds that it is not "fully human" or "authentic." (Note that euthanasia is very different from the decision not to use extraordinary means to preserve life, when the "life" in question is merely vegetative and no longer recognizably human—a point which will be treated in greater detail below. The decision *not to employ* extraordinary means to *preserve* or *prolong* life has a completely different moral character from the decision to take positive action to terminate life by administering a drug which has as its direct and immediate purpose the termination of life.)

There is a serious (but possibly not conclusive) argument which can be made against capital punishment from the same vantage point. The problem of crime is serious, as is the question of proportionate retribution, but is it legitimate to use the life of a criminal in order to solve even these serious problems? Much depends on the judgment one makes about a closely connected question: Can a human being, through criminal conduct, *forfeit* the right to life, and, in this sense of the word, become a mere means to be used in the solution of some other problem? If such forfeiture is possible, then it will be hard to construct a conclusive argument against capital punishment. If the right to life is something which we cannot abandon, even by engaging in the most vicious or depraved criminal conduct, then capital punishment will be difficult to defend.

Closely connected to our right to life is our right of access to the means needed to protect it. The word "access" here is important and it points to the distinction between two kinds of rights which are both real but which must not be confused. Some of our rights are rights to the continued possession of things which we *already have,* either because they belong to us by birth and nature, or because we have acquired them. The right to life is an example of the first, and the right to keep property which one has acquired by fair and just means is an example of the second. Other rights are rights *to acquire* or *to have access to* things which we do not have, but which are either necessary or very useful to us as we try to fulfill the task of becoming human.

These "rights of access" are very real, but they do not imply that other individuals or corporations or governments have the obligation to *give* us the things to which we have such rights of access. These rights of access demand that government on various levels *recognize and effectively promote* our efforts to get them for ourselves. But it is, of course, possible, particularly in a complex society, that the effective promotion of the efforts of people to secure adequate health care will involve governments in setting up and administering health plans and even in providing medical service for its citizens. The question of whether governments should be in the business of providing health care is simply the question of whether, under the circumstances, such action is an apt and appropriate means of securing the basic right of their citizens to such health care.

The right of access to health care is a consequence of the right to life itself, because this latter right includes others—principally the right to defend and preserve life by reasonable means. The word "reasonable" is important here and points to the fact that the particular form of health care to which one has a right of access depends very much on the state of medical science at the time in question, and even on more incidental things like the financial state of the city, state, or national government which may be financing the health care. No one has the right to receive extraordinary or exotic forms of medical treatment which would be so expensive that they would make it difficult for other people to receive even basic medical care.

The right of access to reasonable health care may also include the right to information which is needed to preserve health, and this would imply that dangerous products (tobacco and certain drugs, for example) should be clearly marked, or should be packaged in such a way as to insure that those who cannot make use of this information (children, for example) cannot get at them and damage their health. We also have the right to have food products labeled so that we can be aware of additives and make our own judgments about whether we wish to consume such foods.

Similarly, it may be argued that we have the right to information about other dangerous products which may threaten health—tools, for example, and even automobiles. In all of these cases we have the right, not precisely to be directly protected by government from one or another danger, but the right to *information* so that we ourselves can make informed judgments about the danger and take appropriate steps to minimize it. Human beings do not properly need *keepers,* whose job it would be to watch over them constantly, in order to keep them from hurting themselves, but they do need access to correct information.

In connection with the right to *reasonable* health care, we may also ask whether, in certain circumstances, we also have the *right to die* (that is, the right not to be kept alive artificially, when mere physical existence is no longer a condition for a truly human life). The principle here is not a particularly difficult one to comprehend or to justify, but there are a number of disputed questions about who is to make this judgment, about whether it is binding on hospital personnel, and about what steps should be taken to insure that those who respect the right to die in such circumstances will not be prosecuted either for homicide or for cooperation in suicide.

In such cases, doctors and nurses have the obligation, ordinarily, not to attempt to make moral judgments which are totally independent of the hospital administration; as far as possible they should follow accepted hospital policy. Hospital administrators and staffs have the task of establishing moral guidelines which respect real human values, and they should do this in consultation both with their medical staffs and with their lawyers, so that those who implement these decisions will be free of prosecution or expensive litigation. When such cases come to court, it is important that hospitals and medical staffs file "friend of the court" briefs so that good precedents may be set, and so that state and federal courts may not spend an inordinate amount of time reinventing the wheel.

As noted above, the principle in such cases seems to be clear. When physical life is no longer a condition for living a really human life, and when the patient him/herself makes this judgment and asks that *extraordinary* means to prolong life *not* be used, then hospitals should find ways of acceding to this request. But note that the "right to die" in a human way does *not* include the right to force others to take *positive* steps to terminate one's life.

The case where the patient has suffered irreversible brain damage and exists solely on a vegetative level is more difficult, because here we have to ask who is entitled to make the decision not to continue prolonging life. Again, the principle seems clear. When there is a consensus of responsible medical opinion at the hospital that brain death has occurred, and when even vegetative life would continue only through the use of extraordinary means, then their use should be discontinued. Here, too, the various legal steps mentioned above should be taken, for the protection of the hospital and of the medical personnel.

4.32 Rights of Access to the Material Needs of Life

We have rights of access to things which are necessary for living a fully human life. Foremost among these things would be the "basics"—food, lodging, a reasonable income (or a living wage). Obviously the kind of food and lodging will vary with the time and the place, and the access to employment will have much to do with the character and complexity of the culture and civilization involved. In complex industrial societies, it might even be argued that workers have the right of access to a guaranteed annual wage, because without it they would lack the security which is necessary for a full human life in such a society. As in other such cases, we are talking here about rights of *access*. No one has a right to be given a salary or a house or food as a gift, but we do have a right to be able to get food, housing, and employment if we are willing to work for them (and some means must be provided to make them available to those who cannot work).

We not only have rights of access to material goods. We also have rights of possession over some material things which we have acquired, and this can include both real and personal property. These rights are based on the fact that human dignity seems to be promoted if we can call some things our own and have free disposition of their use.

In general, free market economies (capitalistic systems in one form or another) are built on the premise that the common good is best served when individuals are able to own personal property, real estate, and the means of production, because these enterprises will be managed more efficiently and then all will benefit. Marxism in its various forms has argued that at least real estate and the means of production should belong to society as a whole, on the grounds that this is the only way to keep some people from exploiting others. Obviously no system is completely immune to abuse, but it must be equally obvious to any objective observer today that the various Marxist systems excel in only one respect: the creation of shortages. (In fact, these systems begin to function with some degree of efficiency precisely to the degree to which they abandon doctrinaire Marxist theory and introduce some of the forms of capitalism—particularly competition.)

The right of private property implies that we have the obligation of respecting the property rights of others. These include rights to material goods, and rights to intellectual goods such as patents and copyrights, both of which are ways of insuring that an individual will get a reasonable return on the products which he has worked to produce. These rights and obligations are based on the assumption that when individuals are guaranteed such a return, they will be motivated to be inventive and productive, and this will benefit society at large. (Incidentally, when such rights and obligations are specified by law, one may argue that they exist precisely to the extent to which they are enforceable by law, and to the extent to which those who possess these rights actually do enforce them by law. This principle would be very useful in dealing with problems of copyright law and the piracy of computer software.)

But few rights are absolute. It is important to note that the right to private property (including the right to own the means of production and to hire others to work in them) is conditional. It is conditioned on the premise that such a system of ownership is the one in which the material things of the world (which are really given to us *all*) will most effectively serve us all. It is possible that the day may come when a system which has worked well will cease to function effectively and will have to be phased out in favor of another. Here, too, the principles are clear, but the practical judgments are very difficult, because it is not easy to be certain about the facts and the possibilities in a concrete situation.

Aside from the possibility that an entire social and economic system might some day have outlived its usefulness, it is also possible that a situation could arise in which the apparent property rights of some would interfere with the fundamental rights of others to food, lodging, and employment. In such cases, the property rights of the wealthy and secure must yield to the basic rights of the poor and insecure, and such things as the expropriation of corporations and the seizing of large estates can be justified. This is the case because the right of private property always rests on the premise that the existence of such a right is the best way to insure that the material things of the world serve us all. This premise, though perhaps generally true, may prove to be false in a particular situation, and we have to remain open to this possibility.

Today, moral problems which arise from the existence, on the same planet, of both underdeveloped countries and highly developed countries concern us more than they have in the past, and this is certainly a good thing. But here, as always, to act morally is to act in a deliberately intelligent way, and we have to be wary of noble but simplistic solutions. A very simple way of "solving" problems of inequality of wealth is simply to take wealth from those who have it and distribute it to the poor, but this ordinarily results simply in the spreading of poverty. The best solution will usually be to discover ways of making the wealth of the developed countries even more productive, and to discover ways of motivating these wealthier nations to share with the undeveloped, not precisely their wealth, but rather their skill and expertise in *producing wealth*. We should be very careful in using the word "distribution" in connection with the word "justice." We can learn a great deal from the almost constant disasters in the area of agriculture which seem to be endemic to the socialist and communist economies. What belongs to everybody belongs to nobody, and without the incentive of being able to enjoy the fruits of one's own physical and mental labor, we and our societies remain woefully unproductive.

The right to life and the right of access to reasonable means to protect it include the right not to be manipulated by technology for either scientific or economic purposes. Human beings may volunteer, under certain circumstances, to take part in medical experiments to which they give their informed consent, but they may not be used as guinea pigs to facilitate scientific "progress."

At the same time, it would seem that individuals have the right to choose for themselves forms of medical treatment which have not met with the approval of the medical establishment. Government agencies may well have the task of protecting those who are desperate for a cure for cancer from being duped by con-men and operators. But rather than absolute governmental prohibitions of, for example, laetrile, or other drugs of no demonstrated value, it is the task of government to make sure that those who pay for such treatment are as fully informed as possible.

Something could be said here in general terms about the problems which occur in the field of bioethics, particularly as they bear on the human procreative function. Questions such as *in vitro* fertilization, surrogate motherhood, and artificial insemination are difficult, and we have to keep two things in mind. First, it is probably a good idea to cultivate a certain caution and even distaste for the incursion of technology into the most intimate spheres of human life. Second, if the medical intervention itself is not in some evident way a violation of human dignity and of the basic right to life, it would seem to be allowable, provided that it is essential to some good purpose (such as providing a much-wanted child for a couple who will be good and loving parents).

In all such cases (particularly artificial insemination when the husband is not the donor), it is important to keep in mind that psychological problems can arise which can do a great deal of harm to the marriage itself and therefore to the children who come into existence as a result of such biological interventions. Are there really many cases in which the desire of a couple for a child could not be satisfied by adopting an unwanted child (or one who would have died through abortion)? The publicity which followed the birth of some of the test-tube babies in recent years forces us to ask whether the doctors and the real or surrogate mothers were not seeking fame or notoriety, and it forces us to wonder what the real chances for happiness are for a child who comes into the world in such a situation.

Other experimental work in areas such as gene-splicing should certainly be approached with great caution. However, the work itself is morally neutral, and the mouthing of catch-phrases like "the temptation to play God" does nothing for rational discussion. The question again is whether there is some evident assault on human life and dignity in one or another medical intervention. To respect nature and to accept our status as creatures does not mean to let nature take its course or to do nothing to make the processes of nature serve genuinely human goals. We are called to humanize the world, and the discovery of medical techniques which would, for example, eliminate birth defects and retardation would certainly be a great step in that direction. In this area, we need cooperation between medical personnel and moral theologians, and it is particularly the task of medical personnel to state as lucidly as possible their conviction that one or another form of biomedical intervention does or does not infringe on human dignity.

Of course, the area of biomedicine is not the only one in which there is a danger of being manipulated by technology. Workers can become nothing more than cogs in an industrial machine, and when their work is devalued, the workers' dignity is threatened. To discover ways of enhancing the sense of dignity and accomplishment in work is a moral task of high value. Mere routine is dehumanizing, as is the realization that one's work could be done more efficiently by a machine. The situation is particularly unfortunate when workers feel that they have to resist the coming of the machines (or robots) if they do not want to lose their only means of livelihood. This is a case of clinging desperately to a situation which is basically dehumanizing and which will have destructive effects on all of the human relationships of those involved.

The answer to these problems (which will certainly become incomparably more pressing over the course of the next fifty years) is not retrogressive meddling on the part of government to create "made work" or to promote featherbedding. The answer lies rather in developing an educational system which will prepare people for the creative employment and enjoyment of amounts of leisure time which would be almost inconceivable to us today. If we are liberating great masses of laborers from deadening routine in order to deliver them to the utter passivity of TV's prepackaged pabulum, then a world far worse than that of Orwell's *1984* awaits us in the not-too-distant-future.

The answer to exceedingly complex problems such as these is not to call for the intervention of government on one level or another, since bureaucrats are notoriously inept at solving problems which demand some degree of intelligence. But the glossy rhetoric of *Future Shock* or

Megatrends or the ostentatious antics of people who enjoy running around and babbling platitudes to the effect that "the future is now!" will not help either. We need serious thought by the intelligent people in society on these questions and we need to have them discussed in the major journals of opinion. *Responsible* thought and expression (quite distinct from ventures obviously designed to make money by exploiting an "in" topic or inventing a new one) is a moral task of great value.

4.33 Our Right To Be Responsible for Ourselves

Our human task is to create and fashion a genuine self. We alone are responsible for this and we have the right to exercise our own responsibility, without interference from those who "know better." The assumption is that we *are* capable of exercising such responsibility (in other words, that we are neither infantile nor senile), but this assumption must stand unless there is compelling counter-evidence.

Good questions are being raised today about these problems for perhaps the first time. We are asking, for example, about the right of "society" or of individuals to prohibit the marriage of people who are slightly retarded, or to allow such marriage only on the condition that the parties agree not to have children (or agree to sterilization as a condition of permitting the marriage). The fact that some people regard the passing on of defective genetic material as counterproductive to the aims of society is scarcely sufficient reason to deprive men and women of so fundamental a human right. Similarly, at least in the absence of truly compelling evidence that they have lost the ability to take care of themselves, older people have the right to their independence, as far as this can be safeguarded, and they have the right to privacy, without being treated like children who need to be watched, or like animals who need a keeper. The fact that they may be a cause of worry or embarrassment to their children or others is again no reason to deprive them of basic human rights.

At all stages of our mature adult lives, we have the right to freedom of conscience—that is, the right to make our own judgments about ways of acting which are worthy of being chosen and others which are not, provided our actions do not result in harm to others. This latter proviso *does not imply that all acts which do not harm others are morally good or even morally neutral.* It simply means that we have the right to make our own mistakes and to learn from them. We have the power to create our true selves by acting rightly and well, and this implies that we also have the power to fail in this task of self-creation by choosing poorly. But we cannot enjoy the first unless the second is also granted to us.

Freedom of conscience includes freedom of religion (and indeed it includes all of the personal and "private" rights which are enumerated in the Bill of Rights and which are commonly recognized in the Western democracies today). We will examine these rights briefly below, but here some comments on freedom of religion are appropriate. The Catholic and Protestant nations of Europe were late in recognizing freedom of religion as a basic human right, and Catholic Church authorities really recognized it only at the Second Vatican Council in 1964. Up to that time, many had refused to see freedom of religion as a basic right, on the grounds that religious error has no rights and deserves no protection. But as the Jesuit, John Courtney Murray, had been pointing out for a number of years before the Council, although error has no rights, *persons* do, and one of our basic rights is to do what is in our power to reach the truth about God, about our relationship with

God, and about how God wants to be served, and then to act on the basis of the truth we have found. Our judgments in this matter may be factually erroneous, but if we have done what is reasonably in our power to make them correctly, then we have the right and the obligation to follow them, provided no real rights of others are being violated.

4.34 The Right to Have Others "Stand In" for Us

In the course of life many years pass before we are able to make real decisions, because we have neither the maturity nor the information which are the prerequisites for true freedom. During these years, we have the right to have others stand in for us and make decisions on our behalf. For most of us, our parents do this during infancy, childhood, and early adolescence (and try, at least, to keep on doing it during late adolescence and adulthood). For some of us, the time may come when we are no longer able to make free decisions and to give our lives the shape we want them to have, and this may happen because of poor health of mind or body. And then we have the right to have others stand in for us—sometimes our children, but often friends, doctors and nurses, or others.

This right to a "stand-in" is based on the fact that we are social animals and that we bear real responsibility for each other. When parents fail to assume this responsibility, others must step in, and a number of questions which are raised in medical ethics deal with problems of this kind. Respect for freedom of conscience demands that medical treatment not be forced on the fanatic whose religious beliefs forbid blood transfusions and simple, routine surgery. But respect for freedom of conscience certainly does not demand that we stand idly by and allow fanatical parents to refuse such simple and routine medical treatment for their children. These children have real rights to health care, and neither freedom of conscience nor the basic responsibility of parents to care for their children can be allowed to infringe on the fundamental rights of these children in any way.

This brings up a point which touches on the right to die, which we mentioned earlier in another connection. At the end of life, if we come to the point where we can be kept alive only through the use of very painful and quite extraordinary means, and when we ourselves have lost consciousness and can no longer make the decision to stop using those means to prolong a life which is no longer human, we still have the right to have others stand in for us and make the decision that we ourselves would want to make. And this basic right should be recognized by the courts and implemented in hospital practice.

Policies designed to cope with such cases should be written into the law, and in all such matters it is vital that there be cooperation between the medical community, legislators, and the judicial branch. Moral reflection within the medical community cannot act independently of public law; and if they fail to recognize this, then doctors, nurses, and hospitals will find most of their time taken up with fighting inane lawsuits. Their proper task is to advise the legal community in such matters and to function as friends of the court—and they will do this most effectively *before* the cases come to court.

4.35 Access to Education and Other Cultural Goods

All human beings have rights of access to things or institutions which are necessary for a truly human life. As often noted above, the concrete form which this right takes will depend very much on the level of culture involved and on its degree of complexity. In general, we may say that all members of a given society have rights of access to the information and training which are necessary to function effectively in that society, and the members of that society have the obligation to put at one another's disposal ways of acquiring information and training. But it is fairly obvious that members of remote tribes along the upper Amazon do not have rights of access to secondary education, in the same way in which individuals in American or Western European society might. In the latter societies, secondary education would seem to be the minimum required to be able to function effectively as a member of society, while, in the former, practical training in hunting skills and in the basics of agriculture will be far more useful.

Here, as elsewhere, rights of access to some value or good, although they are real rights, do not ordinarily imply that government or some other group or individual has the obligation to provide those goods free of charge. It is possible that in a functioning society these rights will be used and appreciated more if one pays for the education with money which has been earned by family members or by the individual. But it is also possible that situations may arise in which education will be accessible to most members of a society only if the government provides it or at least subsidizes it. In these matters, moral theologians often invoke the principle of *subsidiarity:* rely as far as possible on the private sector. If and when it fails to do its job, or if the job in question is one which the private sector is ill-equipped to do in the nature of the case, turn first to local government, then to government on the level of the state or the region, and, only if all the preceding fail, to the national or federal government. (This principle is not an expression of hostility to "big government"; it follows from the [generally true] perception that smaller, local government agencies will usually be more accessible and accountable to the citizens, and that the private sector of the economy is usually able to operate in a more cost-effective way.)

In educational matters, it is parents who have the primary responsibility for securing educational opportunities of an appropriate kind for their children, and the schools themselves are a prime area of parental responsibility. Parents, of course, should make their decisions in an informed way, after listening to teachers and administrators, but the supposed (or even real) expertise of educators does not give them the right to preempt parental responsibility.

Some argue today that parental responsibility for the education of their children, coupled with the right of freedom of religion (and of religious formation and education), gives to parents who choose to send their children to religious schools the same right to financial support on the part of the government which they would enjoy if the children were in public schools. This argument seems quite reasonable (though it makes use of a concept of the relation of church and state which is somewhat different from the one which has been accepted up to now in the United States). This view appears to be resisted largely by groups connected with the public schools who fear that their institutions would be deserted en masse by the better students. This may be more interesting as a comment on what teachers and administrators think of their schools than as a rational contribution to the question of government subsidies for religious education (or, more accurately, for *general education which is provided under religious auspices*).

4.36 Political Rights

Under this heading, we include our fundamental right to act as free men/women in creating a human and humane social, political, and economic order. This right includes most of the rights which are found in the Bill of Rights in the U.S. Constitution and in the fundamental laws of other countries which have been modeled on it (and on the French Revolution's "Declaration of the Rights of Man"). The principal rights are those of freedom of speech, freedom of assembly, and freedom of the press. Although most nations in the world today pay lip-service to these rights, they are (with few exceptions) not widely recognized outside the Western democracies, apart from those countries, like Japan, which have adopted the principles of Western political democracy.

The basis of these rights is the fact that the creation of a human and humane society is properly the responsibility of the human being, and that no one, and certainly not the government, has the right to preempt that responsibility. It can be reasonably argued that the forms of freedom mentioned are essential to the exercise of this responsibility. However it is true that this argument, which seems sound enough when applied to the very countries in which the freedom of speech, of assembly, and of the press are recognized, may be flawed when applied to countries in which the population has no experience of the democratic tradition and would be almost totally at the mercy of demagogues of the left and the right.

Even in the Western democracies the rights mentioned are not absolute. All agree that freedom of speech cannot be exercised by standing up in a crowded movie theater and screaming "FIRE!" Most would agree that freedom of the press does not include the right to print known calumnies or to commit slander, while claiming constitutional protection. Most would also agree that the right of assembly (the right to gather peaceably for political purposes, including political protest) does not include the right to interfere with the peaceful exercise of their rights by others (e.g., the right to get an education by attending classes and not having them disrupted by the protesters).

In these matters, the problem is partly that of weighing the various rights which seem to be in conflict, and in the next chapter we will develop some methods which are designed to do just this. But the problem is also that of developing ways of identifying forms of activity which are essentially disruptive, and which therefore cannot claim to be the exercise of real rights. Once these forms of activity are identified, these definitions should be carefully written into the law, and the law should devise means of coping with disruptive activities in a way which makes it possible to distinguish such activities from the exercise of real rights. Provided these principles are recognized, there is no need to worry about the fact that total agreement will never be reached by all sincere and intelligent people in a society.

4.4 SUMMARY

It has been the purpose of this chapter to outline a systematic approach to moral values and to the norms and standards for acting which an individual might follow in the attempt to safeguard and promote these values. The outline is fragmentary, and a number of real rights which are important for the ethical discussion today have not even been mentioned. Among them are the right to privacy and confidentiality, the right to one's reputation, the right to live in a healthy environment, the right to peace on the local and international levels, the right to determine the size of one's family, and many others. As societies grow more complex, cases of real or apparent conflict of these rights among themselves proliferate. Our real purpose has been to indicate the kinds of *questions* which should be raised in the serious attempt to locate rights and to settle cases of conflict. And although some of the principles we have suggested might find rather general agreement, there is scarcely a practical application which would not generate lively debate. And this is a good thing. It is in intelligent and respectful moral discussion that our perceptions of value are sharpened, and that we find our way to norms which are sound in principle and effective in practice.

A final purpose of this "sample system" of values and norms has been to provide us with some concrete data to use as we discuss the question of what to do when real values are in conflict, and the question of how to discover which ways of acting are worthy of being chosen in such cases. These are the questions to which we will turn in the next chapter.

5

Conflicting Values in Theory and Practice

5.1 A DIFFICULT QUESTION

One question has surfaced a number of times in the course of this book: Why do seemingly intelligent people differ in the moral judgments they make about important matters? People seem to disagree not only on practical questions or on cases concerning which they might not know all of the facts; they differ on the question of what kinds of actions are in themselves worthy of being chosen, they differ in their judgments about which actions further and promote the human goal, and they differ in their judgments about what that goal is. The time has come to examine these differences, to ask if they can be resolved, and to look at two additional questions which arise in connection with all of this disagreement.

The first of these new questions concerns the relationship of our moral judgments to civil law. Can we say that it is the task of civil law to promote respect for those values which, in and of themselves, are worthy of being chosen? Can civil law provide a way of solving some of these disputes about values, theoretical and applied.

The second of these new questions deals with

conflicting values in the life of the individual. There seem to be many occasions in life when one and the same choice will promote one or more real values, while violating or destroying other equally real values. In many of these cases we cannot afford not to act, and these cases often confront us with the most serious and difficult choices we have to make. The question is this: When faced with conflicting values, how are we to make a choice?

5.2 WHO CAN MAKE A GOOD DECISION ABOUT MORAL VALUES?

We will begin with a question which we raised in our brief discussion on situation ethics: Who is entitled to make the decision about which ways of acting are *in themselves* worthy of being chosen and which are not? How are disagreements to be settled? Note that this is not a question which can be answered with the airy and irrelevant bit of common nonsense to the effect that "each must make the decision for himself or herself." Obviously each must make his or her own decisions, and this applies both to trivialities like the decision whether to have hamburgers or fried chicken for lunch, as well as to weightier matters such as whether to have an abortion or not. The question is not "Who makes the decision?"—each of us must make it; the question is "Will we make the *right* decision?" And the decision *will* be the right one only if it is based on values which are really there, independently of what we think or feel.

The question of who is to decide about the values which are really there, and about ways of safeguarding them and promoting them, is a serious and difficult question precisely because it is *not* a merely private matter. Such a decision asserts that certain ways of acting lay claim to all of us, simply because we are human, and it asserts that other ways of acting are to be avoided by all of us, simply because they are an affront to our common humanity. But this question about who is entitled to make decisions about these objective values is a good question only if the values are there, objectively, before us and independently of us, and waiting to be discovered. If the values are not there, then the question is meaningless.

Although the question of who decides in such matters is serious and although it will not be easy to find an answer which will resolve all disagreement, this fact should not trouble us unduly, and above all it should not lead us to doubt that the values are there after all. We should face all the difficulties calmly and patiently for a very good reason: the morally good act is not precisely the choice which promotes this or that objective value; the morally good act is the choice *to do all that is reasonably in our power to discover which values are objective. This* choice is within our power; certitude about what the objective values *are* is not.

5.21 Criteria

This means that if we are to answer the question of who is entitled to make these decisions about objective value, we need *criteria* to help us judge whether we and others have done all that is reasonably in our power to discover those ways of acting which are objectively worthy of being chosen. If it is possible to discover such criteria, they will help us decide who is worth listening to, and why, because they will help us judge the genuineness of the commitment to the truth on the part of ourselves and of others.

The assumption here is that when we and others seek the truth honestly and sincerely, we will show this in a number of ways. There will be something in the *content* of what

we say and something about our *way of saying it* which will
reveal the sincerity of our search. The assumption is also
that when we and others are not seeking the truth, we will
betray this fact as well, revealing it in the content and the
style of our assertions and arguments. We need not assume
that the sincerity of our dedication to truth will be obvious,
or that it will be discoverable at all, without careful reflection on our past experience. But the attempt to discover
criteria to determine who is concerned for the truth and
who is not is one at which any person of normal intelligence
can succeed, given time, and this success is a very important
part of moral and personal maturity.

All of these assumptions rest on the insight that the
search for truth is so essential to us, so essentially human,
that we cannot reject it or evade it without leaving certain
telltale signs. They rest on the insight that the denial of
truth and its claims is so fundamentally opposed to the human ideal, so deep a betrayal of our human goal and purpose, that we will not be able to act in such a way without
sacrificing any hope of inner peace and without betraying
this loss of peace in our conduct, in our way of speaking
and our manner of constructing arguments, perhaps even
in the way we look out upon the world, and in the expression on our faces.

5.22 Personality Profile of Those Who Can Make Good Moral Decisions

It will be interesting to attempt to answer the question
of who has the right to make the decision about which values really claim us by attempting to draw a profile of such
a person. (By definition, such a person will be worth listening to as we attempt to make good decisions about the values of life.)

First and foremost, only a person who is convinced that there *are* objective values which are worth discovering is entitled to make such a decision. In the absence of this conviction, moral dialogue is impossible and any talk about human values is an exercise in futility. Any person who is convinced that there are values *there* which claim him/her, and claim *all of us*, is a worthy partner in dialogue, because such a person will make serious efforts to discover those values and will be critical of his or her efforts and those of others.

People who are worth listening to in moral matters will be very aware of the possibility of self-deception—particularly when they are strongly attracted to one course of action, and to the choice or decision which will make this course of action possible. For this reason, they will be self-critical, in the sense that they will carefully examine their own motives, in the sincere attempt to bring any "hidden agendas" to the light. They will be aware of the clever subterfuges that we use to remain in the darkness about certain truths or facts, when we suspect that acknowledging these truths or facts might force us to make some uncomfortable decisions. This attitude is not at all scrupulous or morbid: it is based on an honest assessment of our ability to pull the wool over our own eyes, when we think it is to our advantage, and it is based on the honest admission that there are multiple splits in even the healthiest personality, and that there are many possible "selves" competing for our attention and dedication.

Those who are really convinced of the objectivity of value will have a deep concern for truth and for the facts of the case, particularly if those facts seem to point away from a position dear to their hearts. They will present a strong case in favor of the values which they have discovered, but they will do it in a *reasonable* way, and will be willing to examine opposing arguments and values without feeling threatened by them. Their purpose is not to win arguments, or to appear strong or attractive because of skill in presenting their side of the picture. They will not be pompous or pretentious, and above all will not see facts as a way of scoring points in argument or as a way of gaining control over others. They will be calmly confident that if the truth is given a hearing, the truth will prevail, and they will be very pragmatic in trying to find the most effective methods to insure that the truth does receive a proper hearing. They will not choose ways of presenting the case, and methods of persuasion, which are designed to make them feel noble, or superior, or righteous; rather, they will choose ways of arguing which are honest and which respect the intelligence of their listeners.

Those who are convinced of the objectivity of value will show this in their manner, style, mannerisms, and general deportment. Concern for real value is one aspect of true inner peace. Inner peace does not exclude passionate commitment to value—just the opposite!—but it does exclude vanity, posturing, and posing. With practice, we can come to recognize posing, pretense, pomposity, and fraud, in ourselves and in others, and this is a skill which has great importance in determining who is entitled to make decisions about objective values. But although it takes time and effort to develop this skill, we have a natural affinity for it, simply because we are made for the truth and we have an inborn ability to recognize when we or others stop searching for the truth and decide to remain in the dark.

5.23 Personality Profile of Those Who Cannot Make Good Moral Decisions

Persons who are unwilling to defend the objectivity of value—the fact that there are ways of acting which, in and of themselves, are worthy or unworthy of being chosen, regardless of who knows this and likes this—such persons cannot be partners in moral dialogue. Their positions should be taken seriously and refuted with care, not so that they may be convinced of the error of their ways—they have chosen a position which makes the truth irrelevant—but so that others may not be taken in by their slick rhetoric.

Those who reject the objectivity of value, and who therefore have no right to make decisions about values which lay claim to us all, give evidence of their lack of commitment to value in a variety of ways. Such people have no interest in facts in themselves, and they do not respect facts simply because they are *there;* for them, facts are nothing but tools with which to win arguments and they are tools which may be manipulated and modified at will. Such persons argue in typical ways. If there are no facts to support a point which they wish to make, they are willing to create them out of nothing, but they really prefer to use arguments which are based on prejudice, on mindless emotion, on clichés and on slogans.

Such persons are not interested in *ideas* as such, because an *idea,* in the proper sense of the word, results from the attempt to find the *meaning* of something *real.* They are interested, rather in promoting *ideology*—thoughts and schemes which are not rooted in reality or truth. Such persons are not open to evidence of any kind, and they have no desire to understand the evidence or grasp its meaning. They refuse to deal with the evidence in a reasonable way—that is, to draw reasonable conclusions from it—because they know that such conclusions would force them to be *responsible* for the world, for others, and *above all* for themselves, and they have rejected this responsibility at the start. The overriding motive in the lives of such persons is often *resentment*—resentment at parents or other authority figures, resentment of those with whom they feel that fate has dealt more kindly, resentment of those supposedly responsible for suffering or pain which has been inflicted on them. But this resentment is irrational, and it shows itself in the desire to make others suffer for the real or fancied injuries they have suffered. This kind of resentment leads them to seek scapegoats and to deal in a cruel way with others who are in no way responsible for any harm they have suffered.

Such persons prefer to avoid discussion and argument with intelligent people, because they fear the truth, but if such discussion and argument cannot be avoided, they show their contempt for the truth by "playing to the stands" or by trying to create hysteria to win their points. Their favored form of argument is the attempt to discredit their opponents by irrelevant personal attacks, or by more elaborate smear campaigns, and, most of all, they love slogans which can whip up support in the non-thinking sector of the population.

Persons who reject the objectivity of value are fond of pompous and self-righteous rhetoric, and of posturing and posing, all designed to show how "serious" or "compassionate" or "sincere" they are, how genuine their concern is for "real human beings," and not for "abstract principles" (the term which they prefer for *objective values*). As we have seen, their favorite cliché for rejecting the objective claims which real values make on us is to recite the ultimate platitude in respect to moral decision-making: "In the final analysis, the choice is up to the individual, and no one can make the choice for him/her." (In the context of the moral decision, this truism is irrelevant: no one should ever deny that the choice is up to the individual—who else could possibly make it? But the real question is this: Will the choice which the individual makes respect *values which are really there?* Will it be a choice which does justice to reality, or will it be one which violates the claims of both reality and truth?)

Persons who have no concern for the truth make this evident in many ways, and often their manner and mannerisms betray them—particularly the shrillness and stridency which often appear in their tone of voice and general style. This is inevitable, because we are made for the truth, and we know when we are suppressing our innate need to discover the truth. When we turn against the truth, we violate something fundamental in our nature, and we cannot hide the violence we are doing to ourselves.

5.24 Summary on the Question of Who Decides about Moral Values

The answer to the question is simple: "The man or woman who is acting in a deliberately intelligent way." To act in a deliberately intelligent way is so essential a demand of our common humanity that it will be evident, to the intelligent observer, in our conduct, our deportment, and our demeanor; it will be evident in the way we argue, in our refusal to use mindless emotion as a tool, and, perhaps as much as anything, in the gentleness and lack of cruelty of our humor.

Obviously, people who are convinced of the objectivity of value, and who use all reasonable methods to discover that value and promote it, are not going to make identical value judgments; they never have in the past, and they are not going to start now. But the fact that these values are hard to discover does not invalidate the search for them— it empowers the search, because it is the only condition under which the search can be meaningful. And the calm, serious, meaningful search for value is *itself* the quintessentially good moral act.

However, some good questions still remain. Since our value judgments claim to be objective and assert that they are judgments about values which claim all of us, they cannot be restricted to the private sphere of life; they also touch our lives in community and in society. They touch questions of the organization of society, of appropriate forms of government, and of the role of civil law in the fostering and promoting of human value, and in the defense of real human rights. And this brings us to a second question.

5.3 THE RELATIONSHIP BETWEEN MORAL VALUES AND CIVIL LAW

This question arises precisely because people disagree, often enough, about whether and when personal rights are being violated or infringed upon, and therefore they disagree about what civil law should do about that situation. It also arises because people are unsure about the relationship between legal norms and moral norms, between law, which is a phenomenon of public and social existence, and morality which (particularly in the United States) is regarded as being a private matter, closely associated with one's religious convictions or the lack thereof. Those who make moral judgments in the area of human dignity and human rights are often accused of wanting to force their ostensibly private moral judgments on society at large (and usually those who make this accusation forget that this is just as true in the matter of apartheid as it is in the matter of abortion).

5.31 The Distinct Purposes of Legal Norms and Moral Norms

The purpose of moral norms is quite different from the purpose of legal norms, or, to put it simply, different from the purpose of law. As we have seen, moral norms are judgments which individuals make about values and about the means which are needed to protect and promote them. The purpose of such moral norms is to empower decisions and choices which are morally good because they help us attain our goals as human beings. And we have seen that the fashioning of good moral norms is itself the basic good moral act.

The purpose of both civil and criminal law is not precisely to make us morally good, or to promote morally good decisions in general. These are attractive goals, but law is, as we will see, not an apt and appropriate means to secure their attainment. The purpose of law is much more limited, more restricted: laws are there to prevent us from harming each other and to keep us from acting unjustly toward each other. Law is not designed to protect us from ourselves and its purpose is not to keep us from making morally bad judgments; its purpose is to prevent, as far as possible, suffering which may come to others because of our ignorance, negligence, incompetence, or malice. Law is not an apt and appropriate means of dealing with moral decisions which do not infringe on the real rights of others, and laws which try to do this are simply *bad laws*. Heavy smoking and drinking, homosexual activity between consenting adults, are not *in themselves* the proper object of regulation by law. Of course when the drunk gets behind the wheel, or when homosexual activity involves molestation of children, then law becomes a very appropriate means of protecting the rights of innocent people who can be harmed by such conduct.

5.32 An Important Condition for Legal Norms

When the real rights of innocent parties are being threatened or violated, law will frequently be an appropriate means of coping with the problem. Increasingly severe penalties for drunk driving appear quite effective in keeping these irresponsible menaces off the road. However, law will be an appropriate means to protect the real rights of human beings *only when there is a broad public consensus that real personal rights are being violated.* In the absence of such a consensus, law ceases to be an appropriate means to defend personal rights.

It is important to note the precise point being made here. We are *not* asserting that real personal rights depend for their *existence* on public consensus. This would be an absurd position, because real rights exist independently of who recognizes them or likes them. The question is not that of the *existence* of such personal rights, but of the *appropriateness, the suitability, of law in protecting them.*

5.33 The Moral Evaluation of Actions Not Prohibited by Civil Law

The fact that a particular action or way of acting is not forbidden by civil law, and that no sanctions are imposed on those who choose to act in such a way, does not mean that the decision to act in such a way is morally good or even morally neutral. It means one of two things. Either the way of acting in question does not violate the real rights of others, *or* forbidding the action in question would not rest on the consensus of a majority of the community in which the law would have to be enforced. This does not mean that morality is determined by a majority vote; it does mean that what is legal or illegal in the eyes of the law *is* determined by such a vote, in the sense that a law which does not have the support of the majority is a poor law, a bad law, which will not achieve its goal and which will drag all law into disrepute. Drinking or drugging oneself into a stupor does not become a morally good act simply because it is not against the law. Homosexual activity between consenting adults does not become an authentic fulfillment of our nature as sexual beings simply because the sodomy statutes have been repealed. But such activities, when they remain private, regardless of the *moral* judgments to be made about them, do not evidently and manifestly infringe on the rights of others, and therefore moral theologians generally agree that civil law is not an appropriate means of dealing with them.

5.34 Is There a Moral Obligation to Obey Civil Law?

This second question concerning the relationship of morality to law shows that, although legal and moral norms differ in their purpose, nevertheless the two domains touch at certain points. The question is obviously one which would demand book-length treatment, but it is not out of place to present here the *structure* or outline of the points which might be made in such a book.

It seems fair to say that, in a democratic society, both civil and criminal statutes are generally enacted in order to promote justice and to protect the real rights of human persons. It may even be that in non-democratic societies this is often the case—perhaps more commonly before the democratic form of government came to be accepted as the ideal, but possibly even today. (Although it would be hard to justify the specifically *political* statutes of the communist states, which prohibit their citizens from emigrating or which deny the right to join opposing political parties, many other laws in these countries which deal with non-political crimes would seem to be designed to protect real rights.)

In general, therefore, we might say that obedience to civil law is a practical way of affirming and defending the real rights of others, and of securing a reasonable degree of domestic peace and order. We all have a serious obligation to do what is in our power to prevent general lawlessness or the breakdown of respect of law. The line which separates law-abiding Western societies from downtown Beirut is thinner than we would like to believe, and to the degree to which regular obedience to civil law preserves this thin line, it deserves our support.

Of course, there are some laws which simply impose penalties or sanctions on forms of conduct which are already unworthy of being chosen. The laws against murder, manslaughter, armed robbery, theft, extortion, and other crimes belong to this category, and these laws certainly merit our obedience. On the other hand, laws are always enacted to deal with general situations, and it may be that some of them will make little enough sense in a specific situation. In such cases, violation of the law will probably harm no one. Respect for law in such situations can probably be said to consist simply in being willing to accept the penalty or sanction which is imposed if we are apprehended in violating the law. This is not a case of "it is allright unless you are caught," because what is at issue in such cases is not moral value, but merely a regulation which may not make sense in a particular situation. It is hard to imagine that anyone could normally drive a car through crowded city streets at 70 m.p.h. without being grossly negligent, not only in civil terms, but in moral terms as well. On the other hand, driving at the same speed on rural freeways, where traffic is thin and no one is endangered, does not seem to be a morally reprehensible act, and it is hard to find a moral justification for obeying the 55 m.p.h. limit in such cases.

5.35 Dealing with Unjust Laws

But it is obvious that there are laws in some countries which not only do not protect real rights, but actually violate them. Sometimes the neglect of real rights is blatant, and the laws are written and enforced by power elites who need them to stay in power. There is certainly no obligation to obey such laws, but there is a general obligation to use prudence in disobeying them, because this line of conduct may do more harm than good. In other cases, the neglect or violation of real rights is hidden, not apparent to all, and in these cases, some people are going to become aware of the injustice before others. The question, then, is this: How are those to act who are convinced of the injustice of certain laws, or of the injustice of an entire social and economic system? In general terms, the answer is: by using reasonable, intelligent means to change the laws. Such means include persuasive argument in the public forum, the use of the ballot box and the initiative process. If these methods are not available, then peaceful, non-violent protest is in order, to bring the problem, the injustice, to general attention. In this connection, those engaging in such a protest should understand how important it is to choose methods which do not alienate people, because if they are not careful, they can do great harm to a good cause.

5.36 The Use of Violence

But sometimes none of these means are available. Those who feel the injustice and who perceive it are kept from the ballot box, and peaceful protest is brutally suppressed and has no chance to awaken the conscience of the public. In such cases is violence ever justified? (To cite a practical example: would it not have been desirable to use violence—specifically, assassination—on Hitler and Stalin, and on the higher leadership in both countries about the mid-thirties? Does it not seem likely that untold human suffering could have been avoided by such creative violence?)

The answer in such cases would seem to be a cautious "Yes," but anyone choosing to take this course is bound in conscience to raise the most serious questions and to take the most stringent precautions to protect the innocent. On countless occasions in history, violence in good causes has deteriorated to the point where it has produced greater injustice than that which it was designed to eliminate. Violence has an element of irrationality about it, and this is the root of its power to corrode and corrupt a good cause. In the long run, the perception of precisely this point may turn out to be the key to the moral greatness of both Gandhi and Martin Luther King, although it must be admitted that both were able to appeal to the consciences of the public at large (and especially of the opinion-makers). In Germany and Russia, during the thirties, this was probably not a possibility, any more than it would be in East Germany or Russia today. A treatise on the legitimacy and the limits of violence in just causes is beyond the scope of this book, but some aspects of this question will be touched on later in this chapter.

5.4 ACTIONS WHICH BOTH DEFEND AND DESTROY VALUE: THE PRINCIPLE OF THE DOUBLE EFFECT

The third question to be raised in this chapter is this: When we are confronted with choices in which a single action will create or preserve some real values, while violating or destroying others, how are we to act? Moral theologians always recognized that values might be in conflict in a particular situation, and they developed various principles to try to cope with this problem. It is probably safe to say that the famous principle of the *double effect* was the one most used in the discussion of serious conflicts of value. There is no better way to understand both the strengths and weaknesses of traditional moral theology than to examine the factors which led to the development of this principle. An understanding of how this principle was used and of the motives behind its use can help us find ways of dealing with cases of conflict of value which preserve the worthy intentions of the older approach, without falling into the traps which it could not avoid.

5.41 The Cases for Which the Principle Was Developed

This principle was developed to deal with those cases in which there is a conflict of values, and in which one and the same action seems to be permissible (or even required) from one point of view, and forbidden from another point of view. One might assume that these cases could have been solved by developing a method of weighing the different values and then choosing the greater value; however, this solution was unacceptable to traditional moral theologians, because they argued that certain types of actions were, in themselves, morally bad, and as such could not be chosen. However, cases arose where inaction was as bad as action, and where any choice at all seemed to be at once good and bad. For example, all of these moral theologians were convinced that abortion was wrong in itself, but they asked this question: If the abortion were the unintended by-product of another operation which could be justified on other grounds (e.g., hysterectomy) then might it be permitted, precisely because in such cases it would not be intended in itself?

This type of situation is not uncommon. Our actions usually have many effects, and often one or more of these effects will be "bad" from some point of view. Of course, if the effects of a given action are all "good," then there is no problem in choosing the action; if the effects are all "bad" then it is clear that the action should not be chosen. But life is rarely this simple. (It is assumed in all of these cases that we are aware of the various good and bad effects of the action. If we do not foresee the bad effect in any way, then we are not responsible for that effect as such, although we may be responsible for failing to inform ourselves adequately about the consequences of our actions.)

The words "good" and "bad" are put in quotes here to indicate that the terms were used in the usual, somewhat careless way in this older tradition. Those who developed and used the principle of the double effect usually meant by these terms "objective moral goodness or evil"—concepts which I do not think make much sense. In talking about the principle of the double effect, we will follow their *usage* without accepting the theory which went with it. In other words, we will "let" them speak of *actions* as "morally good" and "morally evil" in themselves, apart from the intention of a human agent. We know that actions in themselves should not be called "good" or "evil," "right" or "wrong," but rather "(un)worthy of being chosen." But the traditional view that there were some actions which in themselves had these moral qualities was so ingrained that these theologians could not shake its effects. This conviction had much to do with motivating the development of this principle, and it had much to do with the form in which the principle was expressed and with its application.

The question which the principle was designed to answer is this: What are we to do when faced with an action which has two or more effects, one or more of which is good and one or more of which is bad? Let us suppose that we are fully aware of both the good and the bad effects. The real problem is this: it is not easy to separate an action from its effects. When we are aware of the effects which our actions are going to have, the action and its effects form a unity, and it is that unity which we choose.

Since the older moral tradition regarded these effects as morally good or bad, depending on whether or not they were in accord with the natural law, this tradition was confronted with the dilemma of an action which was simultaneously good and bad. A typical example is the one alluded to above: a gynecologist has a patient who is suffering from cancer of the uterus and immediate surgery (hysterectomy) seems to be the only way to save her life. However, she is also in the early stages of pregnancy, and the very operation which will (hopefully) save her life will mean death for the not yet viable fetus. The same surgical intervention which saves her life will bring about an abortion. (The assumption here was that saving the woman's life was a morally good act and abortion a morally bad one.)

5.42 The Elements of the Principle of the Double Effect

Moralists approached this difficult case by trying to find some way in which the *intention* of the surgeon and the patient might be prevented from embracing the bad effect—some way in which the bad effect, although foreseen, might be *merely tolerated* and not intended. This development was an interesting one because of the importance it attached to the intention which one had in performing an action. Those who made use of the principle of the double effect still persisted in referring to certain actions in the abstract as "bad" or "wrong," but they were moving toward a most valuable insight: although an action or its effects might be destructive from many standpoints, it was through the *intention* which one had in performing it that it received its distinctively moral qualification.

Note carefully that this does not imply that our intentions are the only factors which need be examined in order to determine whether our decisions are right or wrong. There are actions which *in themselves* are destructive and therefore bad in *some* sense of the word. But we have to remember that "morally good" and "morally bad" are properties, not of actions in the abstract, but of human decision and choice.

But to return to the principle of the double effect: moralists argued that it was possible to keep the intention of the agent from embracing a bad effect which was foreseen, if the following four conditions were fulfilled. *First,* the action which has both good and bad effects is not in itself bad. If it were bad in itself, then one's intention would necessarily reach out to it and embrace it. However, the direct and immediate choice of moral evil is never permitted.

The *second* condition which must be met if an action with both good and bad effects is to be permitted is that the bad effect is not a *means* of attaining the good effect. If it were a means, then there would be no way of preventing the will and intent of the actor from embracing it, because when we want an end or goal, we implicitly want the means to attain it.

The *third* condition to be fulfilled is that the bad effect, although foreseen, is not intended, but is merely tolerated. This is an obvious condition, because the sole purpose of all this sophisticated reasoning is to find a way to keep the intention of the actor from embracing the evil effect.

The *fourth* condition (and probably the one which is

easiest to understand and most difficult to apply) is that there must be a good and proportionate reason for tolerating the bad effect. If the action were performed without such a serious reason, that would indicate a basic readiness to allow evil to happen.

5.43 A Brief Illustration of the Principle

The case which we mentioned in §5.41 above provides a clear illustration of how these conditions might be fulfilled. If there are strong medical indications for a hysterectomy (for example, cancer of the uterus which can be excised before metastasizing), no moral objections can be raised against the action, the operation *in itself*. If the operation in itself were morally questionable, then pregnancy would be quite irrelevant. Second, the "bad" effect (the ending of the life of a presumably nonviable fetus) is not a *means* for attaining the "good" effect (the excision of the cancerous tissue). Third, we can assume in the case that the death of the fetus is not intended—it certainly does not have to be. And, finally, the saving of the life of the mother is at least as important a good as the continuation in life of the fetus. Note carefully that, according to the assumptions in the case, the death of the fetus will be inevitable, and it is an inevitable consequence of the operation. But, although unfortunate, this fact is irrelevant, and the principle of the double effect makes it clear that this is the case.

5.5 SOME FINAL COMMENTS ON THE PRINCIPLE OF THE DOUBLE EFFECT

There were always cases where the principle of the double effect did not apply because the projected action could not clear one or more of the hurdles. In such cases, traditional moralists tried with ever greater subtlety to distinguish the action from its effects, so that the case might be run by again, in the hope that on a second or third try it would clear all of the hurdles. They often tried, within a single effect, to distinguish that element which was really bad from another element which was the means of attaining the good. Other moralists simply counseled the choice of the lesser of two evils, while reminding us of the great possibilities of self-deception which lurk here.

The principle of the double effect was formulated within a moral tradition which viewed certain actions in themselves as morally right and certain others as morally wrong. Once this assumption is made, it is clear that there must be some actions which are simultaneously good and bad, and the principle of the double effect was an attempt to grapple intelligently with this problem. The moralists who developed the principle sensed, correctly, that real moral evil comes about through the *choice* of the individual, and they were convinced that there were no situations in which one could be forced to act in a morally evil way.

The principle of the double effect tried to solve this problem by finding, within the proposed action, an area which was morally neutral, and which could be separated from the bad effects of the action. The principle of the double effect asked whether the intention of the actor could be separated from the evil in the proposed action, but it could do this only by finding some objective distinction between the action and the effect and then concentrating the intention of the actor on this action and on its good effects. However, to separate an action from a foreseen and practically inevitable effect is a very artificial procedure. An action and its foreseen effects usually constitute a global object of choice, and to distinguish between those elements which I intend and those which I willingly allow to happen seems, often at least, less than honest.

But there were two very positive sides to the principle of the double effect: first, it recognized the great importance of human intentions and it implied that a bad intention always made the act morally bad, and, second (although this was not always clear to those who made use of the principle), it tried to find ways of speaking of actions as though they were not in themselves morally bad. But precisely these two points indicate that the principle of the double effect was a sophisticated solution to what was, largely, a pseudo-problem. Moralists assumed that what made a choice or decision evil was the fact that it intended objective moral evil. If they had found other ways to distinguish external actions and had not felt obliged to call them "morally bad" (even though they added the word "objectively" to this phrase), they would have developed more viable and less artificial solutions to pressing problems.

5.6 PRESERVING THE VALUES INTENDED BY THE PRINCIPLE

Even though the principle of the double effect was in some respects flawed, those who devised it and used it were intent on preserving important values. It is important to identify these values and to see how they may be preserved more simply and more realistically, and the first step in doing this is to rephrase the requirements of the principle of the double effect in the more accurate terminology we have developed.

First: the action which has both constructive and destructive effects is not in itself unworthy of being chosen. Second: the destructive effect of the action is not used or intended as a means to achieve the constructive or creative effect. Third: the destructive effect (which, as such, is not worthy of being chosen) is not intended. And fourth: there is a proportion between the creativeness and the destructiveness of the two effects.

This transposition of the requirements into different terms shows something extremely important in the principle of the double effect. The principle was a strong and forceful protest against "consequentialism"—the moral system which insists that any form of activity can be justified on the basis of the good effects or consequences which result from performing it. At its deepest level, the principle of the double effect was a critique of the utilitarian view of human life, which, for example, sees the taking of human life as an acceptable solution to problems of varying degrees of seriousness.

The first of the requirements of the principle of the double effect has precisely this value. It shows us that we must ask not simply about the results or the consequences of our actions, but about whether the proposed action *in itself* is worthy or unworthy of being chosen. It calls upon us to respect the human reality of an action in terms of its own finality. It affirms again that there are ways of acting which *in and of themselves are (un)worthy of being chosen*, regardless of the effects and consequences. Incidentally, this does not mean that we may never choose these actions; in point of fact, they may be the lesser of two or the least of many destructive ways of acting.

The other requirements of the principle of the double effect are also important. The second requirement reinforces this insight and asserts that a way of acting which is under discussion cannot be judged solely in terms of its utility in achieving another goal, but must be judged primarily in terms of its own inherent finality and purpose.

The third requirement of the principle of the double effect reminds us that the destructive effects of our actions are precisely the element which cannot be an object of legitimate choice. The fourth requirement of the principle of the double effect cautions us always to find ways of evaluating and weighing the inherent creativity and destructiveness of our actions.

5.61 More Realistic Questions

It would probably be better to preserve all of these values in a simpler way—something we can do by asking the following questions: Is the action in itself so inherently unworthy of being chosen (because of its own purpose and finality) that no good effect could ever justify it? Do I intend the destructive effects of the action (those aspects which are unworthy of being chosen) either in themselves, or as a means of attaining the good effect? How can I weigh the creativity and destructiveness of the effects, and decide whether the intended creative effect is great enough, serious enough, to justify my tolerating the unintended destructive effect?

5.62 The Intelligent Attempt to Discover Objective Value

Our treatment of the principle of the double effect merits one final comment. The development and the application of the principle show how necessary it is to *think* our way into problems and difficulties and to make a serious attempt to get below the obvious. Serious moral problems cannot be resolved by hasty "gut" reactions. The decision to "do what I feel is right" is pointless and irresponsible, unless I have taken intelligent steps to insure that what I feel is right is the result of my best efforts to discover the objective values which are at stake.

5.7 SUMMARY

In this chapter we began by asking who is entitled to make morally good judgments about the real values in life, and we concluded that those who accept the objectivity of truth, and the validity of its claims on all of us, are the ones who have the right to make such decisions. Second, we discussed the role of civil law in relation to private and public morality, and we concluded that, although morality and law are related, they have very distinct purposes. Third, we discussed the traditional method of solving cases where values seem to be in conflict—the principle of the double effect—and we concluded that there are simpler ways of solving such problems—ways that they become available as soon as we stop talking about actions *in themselves* as being morally good or bad.

6

Ethical Choice
and Christian Faith

6.1 IS THERE ANY CONNECTION BETWEEN CHRISTIAN FAITH AND THE MORALLY GOOD LIFE?

Much of what has been said up to this point could easily be found in a textbook of philosophical ethics. We have tried to present an intelligent analysis of the conditions of human decision-making—an analysis which might appeal to reasonable men and women, regardless of their religious convictions or the absence thereof. Most of the points made do not appear to be distinctively theological: the word "God" has been used rarely; there has been almost no discussion of sin or faith; and although the Old and New Testaments have been alluded to occasionally, neither has been used as a source of guidance for ethical choices which would be distinctively Christian. We have tried to analyze the process of human decision-making in an intelligent and reasonable way and would be quite happy if the atheist could accept most of what has been said.

But this very fact raises some serious questions. Does faith really play a role in the ethical choices of the Christian? Or can faith safely be relegated to the domain of feeling, so that the Christian must make his or her choices on the same philosophical or humanistic basis as everyone else, whether non-Christian or non-believer? Is the concept of sin out of date—a relic or vestige of the period before mankind came of age? Should we speak instead of choices and decisions which are unfortunate or impractical and talk of the social, economic or historical circumstances which force people to act in this way and which are responsible for their errors in judgment? Are the Old and New Testaments relevant to the contemporary world and to the moral choices which we are called upon to make in that world?

In a somewhat different vein we might ask these questions: Is belief in God, or perhaps even Christian faith, necessary for the good moral act? On this latter point the dilemma is obvious. If faith is necessary for the good moral act, then the overwhelming majority of human beings who have ever lived are, at best, moral infants, and, at worst, moral lepers. But if faith is not necessary for the morally good act, this would imply that humanistic and philosophical considerations are the only ones which are relevant to the making of an ethical decision, and it implies that faith should be relegated to the area of ritual and of personal feeling.

6.11 A Peculiar Tension

We can answer these serious questions if we examine a most peculiar tension, even contradiction, which characterizes the human situation. There are two undeniable facts about the human animal which seem to be mutually exclusive. The first fact is the point which we have labored to make throughout this entire book. On the deepest level, the morally good act is the admission that truth and value are objective, and it is the commitment to seek them with all of our power. We are made for truth and value and we have a natural desire for them. This desire is central to our being, and it functions as a constant critique of our judgments about truth and value: in important matters, we will sooner or later find truth and value if we give free rein to our desire for them.

Of course, there are obstacles to the discovery of truth which may make that discovery come later rather than sooner. Many of these obstacles simply reflect our limitations, and they are a sign that the discovery of the truth about our human situation takes place gradually in human history and not once and for all in the life of each human being. This fact does not contradict the human commitment to value and it does not involve moral evil.

But there is a second fact which seems to exclude the one mentioned two paragraphs above: although we are made for truth and deeply desire objective value, at least at times we refuse to search for the truth and refuse to recognize objective value. Instead of thinking correctly so that we can choose rightly, we choose wrongly and try to make our thinking conform to this morally bad choice. We rationalize, trying to convince ourselves that we are not acting destructively, although we know that we are.

There is something exceedingly strange at work in this paradox, this tension, and this contradiction. There is a discrepancy between an "is" and a "should be" which seems to contradict the very nature of our power to seek the truth and do it. Something is wrong, not in order, at the center of the human personality. It is not simply that we are limited, or slow in discovering the truth; it is rather that we turn away from the truth. Paul put it simply in Romans, chapter seven: "The good which I would like to do, I do not do. What I do is the evil which I hate." What we are facing here in all of its simplicity and all of its depth is the problem of evil.

It is clear that no one chooses evil *as* evil (or, in the terms we have insisted on in this book, no one chooses to destroy value simply for the sake of destroying value). Non-value and destruction must first be masked as value before we choose them; but it is in this most fundamental of choices—the choice to let falsehood and destruction wear the mask of truth and creativity—that real evil lies.

The tendency to act in this way is the very heart of what the Christian tradition has called "original sin": not a personal act, but something very much like a power or force which impels us to reject God and the truth of God and to substitute for it a lie of our own making. But in yielding to this tendency, we become really, personally guilty, because, although we know that we are made for the truth and called to it, we deliberately suppress it (and a sign of our deliberation is that we try to suppress the awareness of what we are doing, even from ourselves). Paul speaks of this situation with great power in Romans 1:18–31. He traces all human pride, deception, and unpitying hatred to the fact that "although men knew God they did not treat him as God and did not give thanks to him, but they made fools of themselves so that their senseless hearts were darkened. They thought that they were wise but they were fools . . . and they exchanged the truth of God for falsehood" (vv. 21–23). Original sin is a tendency, but it is one which we all ratify, and in ratifying it we sin.

6.12 Original Sin

To speak of original sin is not, of course, to argue for the historicity of the myth of creation and of the fall of

Adam and Eve; it is simply to take seriously this destructive tendency in human nature. A careful and honest observation of human nature leads to the conclusion that there is something wrong or flawed with human beings as they exist, and that the human animal must be overhauled before we can create the selves which we are called to create, before we can discover the truth and do it. The Christian message offers precisely such an "overhaul," such a re-creation of the human being. For Mark, the "good news" which Jesus brings is precisely the proclamation that God accepts us unconditionally, and that this gives us the power to become the persons he wants us to be. For Paul it is the "good news which works for the salvation (healing!) of all" in Romans 1:16 which achieves this effect. In John 8:32 it is the "truth (which) will make you free."

The Christian message claims to make authentic ethical decision possible, and from the beginning Christians have been urged to make good moral decisions. Paul often expresses this imperative in the form "live according to the gift which has been given to you"—that is, act like those persons who you really are. This poses an interesting question: Is there a special *content* in Christian ethics? Are there certain actions which Christians must either perform or avoid simply because they are Christians? Does the revelation of the Old Testament or the New Testament prescribe or forbid certain actions? These questions have been answered by Christians in different ways, even though all Christians are convinced that the Christian message and the faith which is a response to it have an overwhelming influence on our ethical decisions. But what is this influence, and how does it function? To answer this question, we will turn to what we have called "a peculiar tension" in human nature, and to an aspect of that tension which has traditionally been called "sin."

6.2 THE TRADITIONAL APPROACH TO THE PROBLEM OF SIN

As in so many other areas of ethics and moral theology, there is an older, more traditional approach, which has a more superficial or external relation to Scripture, and a more modern one which draws heavily on a critical reading of the New Testament. The older approach was accepted for several centuries, and has certain characteristics which are typical of the Counterreformation period, although its roots are much older. The newer approach has been gaining ground since Vatican II, although it is really based on the critical exegesis of Scripture, as this developed in Protestant university theology in Germany in the late nineteenth century and throughout the twentieth century up to the present, and among Catholic scholars, from very tentative beginnings at the end of the nineteenth century, to the point today, where critical exegesis, although by no means accepted by all, is the touchstone which distinguishes serious theology from various parodies which usurp its name.

We will discuss this newer approach in later sections of this chapter. But we will begin by outlining the characteristics of the older approach—an approach which, although moribund, is still fairly widespread. The older or traditional approach to the question of what is distinctive in the ethical choices of the Christian rests on three convictions—the conviction of the reality of sin, the conviction that God, through his law, makes objective demands on human beings, and the conviction that one of the basic functions of the sacraments (if not the principal purpose) is to enable human beings to fulfill the demands of God's law.

6.21 Baptism and Original Sin

This older approach had a very definite understanding of the sacrament of baptism and of original sin. Original sin was understood not as a universally corrupting tendency or drive, but rather as the loss of grace, the deprivation of a state of union with God. "Grace," understood here as a share in divine life which was consequent on man's union with God, had originally been lost by Adam, our first parent, and with the exception of Jesus (and, as would be said during a later period, Mary), all human beings inherited this loss or incurred this deprivation, simply because it was passed on in the procreative process. Although original sin was removed by baptism, it left strong traces—that is, certain inclinations or proclivities to sin. These were generally summed up under the technical term "concupiscence"—a term which, as Thomas Aquinas used it, meant any and all of the disordered strivings of human nature, but which, because of its etymology, was in practice often restricted to those forms of sexual desire for which the theology of the day could find no justifying excuse.

6.22 Obedience to Law

Further, the morally good act was defined and understood as one which was made in obedience to those laws which were, directly or indirectly, God's laws. The Old and New Testaments were regarded as the source of new laws which would not have been known to human beings unless they had been revealed. Scripture was therefore primarily the revelation of God's law—the Ten Commandments in the Old Testament, the Sermon on the Mount, or something called more generally "the law of Christ." Furthermore, in virtue of Jesus' words "he who hears you hears me" and "whatever you bind on earth will be bound in heaven," the Church acquired the power to further specify the law of God, and even to make new laws. In fact, it was quite common in moral theology to speak of the Old Testament, the New Testament and the teaching of the Church as clarifying, specifying and determining the exact meaning of the natural law. Those who held this view thought that there were many areas of human life where we can only learn to act ethically and morally by turning to revelation and to the Church as the interpreter of revelation. What this meant practically, according to those who held this view, was that the Church could impose quite distinct and concrete obligations, and this was a very common Catholic interpretation.

6.23 Sin as the Violation of Law

In this traditional approach, since sin was, by definition, a violation of God's law, it became extremely important to specify the various types or categories of sin, and the degree of seriousness of each. The fact that traditional moral theology in the Catholic Church had developed primarily to train priests for the hearing of confessions and the fact that the Council of Trent had asserted that sins must be confessed according to their type and their relative gravity, both played a very important role.

Sin was understood as a violation of God's law, and some sins were seen as a violation of the natural law, while others were seen as violations of the divine positive law— the Ten Commandments and the laws presumably given by Christ or others in the New Testament—and still others were seen as violations of the laws of the Church. (The term "positive law" here means "law made by God in a distinct act subsequent to creation.") The relative gravity or seriousness of the sin was determined by ascertaining whether it was a violation of a serious law of God (in which case it was a serious or "mortal" sin) or a violation of a not-so-serious law of God (in which case it was a minor or "venial," pardonable, sin). The question of determining which of the laws of God were serious and which were not was settled by the consensus of moral theologians and occasionally by the intervention of Church authorities. This whole situation led to a view of sin which saw it very much as an action rather than a stance, and it led to a view which did not always distinguish clearly between the decision and the external action which might follow upon it.

6.24 Problems with the Older Approach

There were serious problems with this older or more traditional approach, and they have been brought to light by two important events. The first is the development of a solid, critical exegesis of the Old Testament and the New Testament, and the second is the development of better insights into the decision-making process—insights which we owe to the work of depth psychology and psychoanalysis. These developments have had a profound effect on our views of sin and its relationship to law.

Original sin has been demythologized. We are aware now that most of the Adam and Eve story belongs to a common body of myth which was circulating in the ancient Near East for centuries before its incorporation into the Old Testament. Furthermore, its incorporation into the Old Testament was not the attempt of naive primitives to write primeval history, but rather the attempt of a highly sophisticated theologian to state in mythical form some profound truths about the relationship of God and human beings. Original sin was not an action on the part of one human being at the beginning of history, nor is it an hereditary infection. It is rather a condition or situation in which human beings find themselves—one which, to be sure, they are called upon to resist and surmount, but hardly one which could be described as the deprivation of a previous state of union with God.

The change in thinking about original sin resulted in a new view of baptism and of its function. The sacrament does not drive out the devil or terminate a state of enmity with God, and it does not in some magical way create a state of union with God through an infusion of divine life. For the adult, it is the external, ecclesial symbol of saving faith. For the infant, the real grace of baptism (grace, that is, in the sense of effective divine favor) touches the commitment of the parents and of the whole Church to create for the child being baptized a situation in which faith and love become practical possibilities.

It has become evident that, at least from the standpoint of the New Testament, God is not an arbitrary lawgiver who sets up regulations as tests of obedience and then demands conformity to these essentially impersonal norms. It has become clear that, whatever its philosophical validity, the concept of natural law (a term which has assumed widely different meanings in the course of history) is largely a development of medieval and early modern thought and cannot really be found in the Old Testament or the New Testament. The exegesis of precisely those texts in Paul's letter to the Romans, which were thought to support natural law theory, has made this evident. Furthermore, studies in history and anthropology have made it eminently clear that the "natural law," as it developed in the centuries after Thomas Aquinas, lacks much of the clarity and certainty which it was so readily assumed to have in an earlier age.

In respect to divine positive law, good exegesis of the text of the Ten Commandments makes it clear that we are dealing there with later constructions on the part of those who shared the Yahweh faith. In content, much of the material of the Ten Commandments and of most of the Levitical and Deuteronomic traditions coincides with Semitic customary law, as we find this exemplified among other peoples of the Fertile Crescent during their late nomadic period and early period of settlement. When we turn to the New Testament, we find that there is growing agreement today that Paul's words in Romans 10:4 ("Christ is the end of the law") refer not simply to the law of Moses, but rather to any and every religious law which would attempt to regulate the relationship between human beings and God on the basis of obedience or disobedience to that law.

In regard to sin, the traditional approach failed because it emphasized action (and very often *actions,* conceived in a kind of isolation from the person performing them) at the expense of the stance taken by the actor and at the expense of the overall direction taken by his/her life. In practice, if not in theory, sin was discussed apart from the kind of person one was becoming, and apart from the kind of person one wanted to be. As long as sin was conceived of as the violation of law, the distinction between mortal and venial sin implied, first, that God was a lawmaker, and, second, that his laws came in only two fundamentally different types: those which were serious and those which were not. This led of necessity to the attempt to identify those sins which were serious and to do this as exactly as possible, so that one might take all prudent steps to avoid mortal sin. This careful calculation led, in turn, to the question of exactly how far one could go in a given area of human endeavor without falling into mortal sin.

But these attitudes trivialized sin and reduced it to the level of a pre-personal taboo. In the process it was easy to fall into the practice of "keeping accounts with God"—that is, of calculating the performance of "good works" and noting how often one avoided actions which would violate one law or another, and doing all of this in a way which would have made a Pharisee blush. For the Catholic, confession was understood as the sacrament in which serious sins were removed, and through which one returned to the "state of grace"; and it seemed quite possible to jump in and out of mortal sin and the "state of grace" several times a week and perhaps even in the course of a single day. In order to make sure that confession really "worked," it was not uncommon to go over lists of sins before one received the sacrament, to make sure that no sins had remained undiscovered, and then at the end of confession to accuse oneself of "all the sins I cannot remember," so that God would have nothing of which to accuse us and all our tracks would be covered.

Obviously, even in the old days, neither sound theology nor serious catechetics condoned practices like these, but the view of sin as the violation of law, which was then almost universal, made such developments and practices hard to avoid, and made it difficult for those confessing their sins to raise the question of the fundamental relationship with God which was manifesting itself in all of their actions.

All of these problems arose out of the attempt to answer the question of the relationship of Christian faith to the moral life of the Christian and to answer it in one specific way—that is, by defining sin as the violation of law, by seeing Scripture as the source of law, and by viewing the sacraments as ritual acts, designed primarily to cope with the violation of law. It seems clear that the question of the relation of Christian faith to our ethical choices must be raised again. There has to be another way.

6.3 ANOTHER APPROACH TO THE PROBLEM OF SIN

A second and very different approach is possible. This approach sees the ethical decision not as one which results from obedience to law, but rather as one which is truly intelligent, because it springs from a thoroughgoing commitment to reality, to the real world. In this approach, Christian faith and the Christian message influence ethical decision, not by providing new laws or norms, but rather by bringing about a fundamental change in the human situation, by "overhauling" the human being and giving him/her the power to think and act in a truly intelligent way. In this new approach, it is faith which makes it possible for us to be intelligent in thought and in action. This approach will enable us to keep what is solid in the tradition, while avoiding some of the difficulties with which that tradition did not adequately deal. Even more importantly, it will do justice to the New Testament evidence.

6.4 A GIFT GIVEN

This last point is of great importance: the New Testament is not the demand to obey a new law; it is the good news of something which has happened, the good news of a gift which has been given, and the good news of the effects of that gift in human life and action. The imperative mood is by no means absent from the New Testament, but it is not an imperative which expresses itself in the enumeration of prescribed and prohibited actions; it is not law. The Christian message is a word which *alters* the situation of human beings, liberating them from those forces and factors which keep them from discovering the truth and doing it.

6.41 A Changed Situation

We can begin by making some general observations concerning what the Gospels say about Jesus' words and actions, and about how these words and actions are related to law. For before it is anything else, the Christian message is the message of and about Jesus; it is the good news that in this man God has acted in a decisive and definitive way—in such a way as to change the human situation and to redefine what it means to be human.

God's action in Jesus confers on us new and unrealized possibilities by removing obstacles to intelligent action. The place where we stand is no longer the same. The world is different. For us human beings on our own, the world is the place in which we affirm ourselves against nature and neighbor. It is the sphere in which time will eventually triumph over us. It is the sphere in which we affirm our alienation from a "god" whom we perceive to be a threat to our integrity and our freedom. But Jesus redefines the words "God" and "world." The words henceforth have different meanings, and the realities behind the words are different. The world and life are gifts, and time is no longer a threat. Christian faith empowers a new relationship to the past, the present and the future. And *we* are different, because the word "God" no longer means what it did. God has come to share our destiny in the world, and there is nothing

in the world which can alienate us from him and from ourselves.

Jesus *describes* this new situation in the language of his
day, using all of the idioms which were current at the time.
If we insist on ignoring these idioms, we will preclude all
possibility of understanding his description. Jesus asserts
the absoluteness of God's claims by using Semitic turns of
phrase ("Unless a man hate his father and his mother . . . ").
He asserts the totality of God's gift in parables of the kingdom which speak of a feast to which all are invited, or of a
harvest which exceeds all bounds. But Jesus not only describes the new situation; in his life he lives out the gift and
the claim of God, acting as though he implicates God in
everything he does, and offering, in God's name, unconditional acceptance to all at the very moment in which he
claims them just as unconditionally. Jesus is continually saying, in word and in action, "You thought you knew what
the word 'God' meant, and you thought you knew who you
were, but you were wrong on both counts: things are infi-
nitely better than you could ever dream."

6.42 A Place for Law?

However, there seem to be passages in the New Testament which call into question the interpretation given
here. There are places in which Jesus seems to be imposing
a new law (that is, a binding precept or prohibition) which
is laid down as a condition of entry into eternal life. Texts
such as Matthew 5:17ff and Matthew 5:21ff are to the point
here, as well as Jesus' admonition to the apostles: "Whatever you bind on earth will be bound in heaven." Churchmen have traditionally appealed to this text as giving them
the right to make laws which bind in conscience. But these
texts can be interpreted in another way, and it is becoming

clearer all the time that they must be. Jesus called upon his hearers to act in accordance with the demands of their new situation, to act like the new selves which they now were. There is no doubt that he made this demand, and when he reminds his listeners about who they really are, he tells them to *become* just that in practice. His moral demands are serious and they are absolute, but they are not law for a very important reason.

Law would list the actions and omissions which God demands or punishes and it would list those performances which we would have to achieve in order to be in good standing with God. But according to Jesus, God does not demand or prohibit certain actions; rather he lays claim to the whole person. The person who accepts this claim has to be reminded of just what this acceptance involves, so that his/her acceptance of God's claim will be real, but this reminder is not the imposition of a new law. Even in a text like that of Matthew 5:21ff, Jesus is not really laying down conditions of entry into eternal life, nor is he providing us with a measurable norm by which we can know whether or not we have merited heaven. Rather, he is implicitly asking us if we have grasped who we really are, now that we have begun to respond to this invitation. What we have here is a statement of our identity, and a plea to become the ones who, in a sense, we already are. Jesus is continually answering the question: "What does it mean to really hear the good news?" For Jesus, acting is not something which follows on hearing. Rather, acting *is* hearing, and this applies above all to that most human form of hearing: deciding.

6.43 A Note about Jesus' Teaching on the Law

Jesus' teaching on the law is a very important part of the Sermon on the Mount (in Matthew, chapter 5) and it is also the source of some of the most troubling statements which Matthew's Gospel attributes to Jesus. In Matthew 5:17–19, Jesus seems to raise the question of the permanent validity of the Jewish law, and he apparently takes a very conservative position. This section is found only in Matthew's Gospel, and it raises a good question: Did Matthew intend these statements as a rejection of Paul's teaching on the law (Rom 10:4)? And if so, had Matthew understood or misunderstood Paul?

There is no real evidence that Matthew was trying to refute Paul, but it seems clear that he was taking a position which is irreconcilable with Paul's own. In these verses we have a clear example of the *judaizing* tendencies of Matthew and his community—that is, their intention to impose a Jewish Christian interpretation on Jesus, and one which gives us not the words and thoughts of Jesus but those of his *interpreters*. In this view, Matthew would be the spokesman for a Jewish Christian community which did not yet see the incompatibility of the Gospel and the law. This interpretation raises the question of whether there could be real disagreement between Matthew and Paul on a matter of major importance. It therefore suggests the possibility that the New Testament contains not only the word of God about who he is, but the word of God about who we are, and that this latter word includes the revelation of our (here: Matthew's) misunderstanding of God's word and of our resistance to the real Jesus. Radical and even troubling as these suggestions are, I believe they are the only way to interpret the verses in question.

6.44 Metanoia

But what could it possibly mean for a Christian to *become* what he/she *is*? This process is referred to by the verb "metanoein" in the Greek New Testament. As a noun, it is sometimes translated as "penance" or "repentance," but neither translation is very accurate. The word really refers to the act of turning away from an old world, an old self, and the turning toward a new world and a new self. Jesus himself spoke, in the idiom of his day, of "denying self," and his words have often been used to justify various ascetic practices of "self-denial," but Jesus' words really have nothing to do with such ascetical exercises. What Jesus demands is a resolute rejection of that false self which is defined by self-assertion at the expense of others. What he demands is the willingness to accept the self as the gift of God and not as the product of our own self-aggrandizing drives. This is really the same as believing in the good news which he preaches: the good news that we are accepted by God and that the fullness of life is something which we receive as a gift and not something which we can effect through our own endeavors. Jesus joins the themes of metanoia and good news when, at the beginning of his public life, he demands of his hearers: "Change your way of acting and believe in the good news." The two are the same.

This turning away from the old world and the old self and from the destructive structures of both is a turning toward the real God, the real neighbor and the real self. It is the coming-to-be of a new relationship with God, with the world, and with one's own self—the relationship which is called "love." God is no longer the tyrannical "supreme being," to be placated and manipulated; he is the Father, whom we trust absolutely and from whom nothing can separate us. The neighbor is no longer an object to be controlled, but one whom we can affirm and whose authentic existence we can promote. This affirmation is a thoroughly realistic act, and, in the concrete, it may involve commitment to discipline, control, restraint, and even the use of force. A Christian *may* renounce the use of force, but he/she does not have to. It is hard to tell what the historical reality was behind the Gospel accounts of Jesus' driving the money-changers from the temple, but as presented in the Gospels, it is a violent enough scene.

Jesus' preaching points out the structure of metanoia, and therefore of love, but he does not offer a concrete program. For example, his words in Matthew 5:38–42 tell us, in typically Semitic fashion, not to seek vengeance. They tell us that the epoch ruled by the law of retaliation ("an eye for an eye, a tooth for a tooth") is over and done with. On the other hand, Jesus' words do not tell us that we may not recover damages when we have been treated unjustly, or that we may not insist that our rights be respected. And they do not tell us to let the unjust assailant have his way with us or with others.

Jesus offers no social, political, or economic plan for ridding the world of oppression. He seems to have had friends among the rich and the poor, among the law-abiding and the law-despising. To the dismay of modern activists, there are no signs in Jesus of any desire to campaign against institutions, or against military and economic oppression, slavery and the like. Rather, Jesus lays claim to the total person and wants to liberate the whole human being. He seems to feel that if this is done, then everything else will take care of itself.

The so-called "commandment of love" is not a commandment at all. (Can love really be *commanded?*) It is a *description* of the new man/woman who has turned away from the false and destructive self to the true self. Our love of God is our acceptance of the one who is *for* us without bound or reserve; it is our act of "letting God be God." Love of neighbor becomes possible for us when we accept life as gift. Love of neighbor is not commanded by God in the sense that we could *use* the neighbor as a way of fulfilling the command of God, or in the sense that we might "look through" the neighbor and see only God. Both of these approaches demean and degrade the neighbor to the level of a thing which we might use in order to correctly arrange our relationship with God.

6.5 THE SERMON ON THE MOUNT

Jesus' sermon in the fifth chapter of Matthew's Gospel is often treated as the sum and substance of his moral teaching (or, more accurately, the post-Christian world enjoys paying lip-service to it in occasional fits of pious nostalgia). This would be an appropriate place to sum up the comments we have made on Jesus' preaching and on their relevance for our ethical choices today.

In words which seem, superficially, to be a new law and a new commandment, Jesus *describes* in this text the person of faith. To live in the way that Jesus describes is a sign that one accepts the new understanding of self which he brought. This new way of existing is not the fulfillment of new obligations which might be discovered by faith; it rather *is* faith—the continued act of letting God be himself, letting him be the one he wants to be for us.

Jesus' description is not law, because, unlike law, it does not claim our *actions* (as though it commanded some and forbade others). Rather, it lays claim to *us*, in our entirety as persons. Jesus' description of existence in faith is highly idiomatic, and it can be decoded and understood only by one who is aware of the idioms. Furthermore, the Sermon on the Mount, in its present form, is a construction of Matthew, and we have to be very cautious in claiming that any of these words go back to Jesus himself.

Christian existence, as described in the Sermon on the Mount, is characterized by unbroken reliance on God and not on oneself or on any other inner-worldly structures. The real point of the "happiness sayings" ("Beatitudes" is a hopeless translation!) is that the very situations which are, in the judgment of the world, the mark of failure can awaken us to the nearness of God if we only let them. Even better: God approaches us in those situations, if we are attentive to his presence. When our existence is unsupported and the props are gone, then we are in a position to feel the presence of God; when the world fails us, God will not. And this unbroken reliance on God has immediate effects on the way we deal with each other; the Christian who is accepted by God is freed to accept the neighbor as wholeheartedly and unconditionally as he/she is accepted by God.

6.6 CHRISTIAN ETHICS ACCORDING TO PAUL

Paul's ethical reflection (like everything else in his life) is determined by two factors which were all-important in his view of the relationship of God and human beings. The first is often translated as the "justice" or the "righteousness" of God, but neither of these translations is very good. What Paul is really speaking of is God's act of *asserting his rights over the world,* his act of *claiming the world and us as his own.* The second factor is what Paul calls "faith"—not the uncritical acceptance of statements which others tell us are true, but, rather, the act of *willingly allowing God to assert his rights over us,* the act of *letting God claim us as his own.* To do this is to accept the new definition of the words "God" and "human being" which became real in Jesus, and this is pre-cisely what it means to accept Jesus as Lord.

The fact that Jesus is Lord implies, and, in a certain sense, imposes, *a new way of acting*, and it is here that we touch on Paul's teaching of the relationship of faith to eth-ical activity. Since the time of the Reformation, this ques-tion has been the source of many disputes between Protestants—particularly Lutherans—and Catholics. The discussion has centered on the problem of the relationship of faith to our own good works in achieving salvation—the right relationship with God, now and for eternity. If we substitute the expression "ethical decision" for "good works," it is obvious that we are dealing here with a ques-tion of prime importance for this book.

The faith/works debates of the Reformation period and after often led both Catholics and Protestants to one-sided and distorted positions. Sometimes Catholics spoke of faith in a way which made it into little more than the ac-ceptance of dogmatic, moral, and even ceremonial laws. Sometimes Protestants spoke of faith in a way which made it into the acceptance of the *doctrine* of justification by faith alone, thus obviating the need for, and effectively paralyz-ing, ethical activity. Neither of these positions is held by competent Catholic or Protestant theologians today. ("Competent" theologians are defined here as those who care about what is really being asserted in the New Testa-ment and who are acquainted with ways of discovering what the New Testament teaches.)

However, we frequently encounter today, on the part of both Catholics and Protestants, an interpretation of faith and of its relation to ethical activity which should be men-tioned here. In the view we are alluding to, faith is seen as "showing" or "expressing" itself in good works. At first sight, this seems to do justice to that very large number of texts in which Paul exhorts his hearers to ethical activity: for example, 1 Corinthians 7:19: " . . . what counts is keeping the commandments of God." And Galatians 5:6: " . . . faith which is activated in love is what counts." Cf. also 1 Corinthians 13:2 and 1 Corinthians 9:24–26. However, I believe that to interpret these texts as demands to manifest faith by obeying the law, or precepts, or commandments, is inaccurate and even dangerous. To interpret them this way implies that faith confronts us with a demand or a call to act in a certain way. The further implication is that if we *do* act in this way demanded by faith, then we have achieved or accomplished something of which we can boast, and which can ground a claim *against God.* ("I have done my part, God; now you do yours: give me the appropriate reward.") Obviously this interpretation strikes at the heart of Paul's teaching on faith.

There is a much better way of speaking about Paul's view of the relationship of faith to ethical activity—one which is not subject to this danger, and one which, at the same time, does justice to those texts of Paul in which he exhorts his hearers to act rightly and well. This approach keeps in mind the fact that faith is the decision of the human being to "serve a new Lord," to belong to a new sphere of influence, a new domain—that of Jesus Christ.

Faith is the act of choosing to serve Jesus as Lord, the act of bringing all of the determining factors of one's life under his control. In this sense, faith *includes* a new definition of self and a new scale of values. It is not as though we are first called upon to believe, and only then faced with a moral challenge which is consequent on this belief. The process is very different: the free and deliberate hearkening to God's word in Jesus Christ already, in itself, includes a new way of understanding and acting. If this new way of understanding and acting is absent from our lives, this does not indicate that we have failed to express our faith; it is rather a sign that our faith itself has been less than a whole-hearted welcoming of the Lord Jesus into our lives. In such a case, faith is deficient, weak, *in itself*, and not because it has failed to have effects distinct from itself.

We are saved by faith alone, because faith is the only channel through which the lordship of God in Jesus Christ is effective in us. To act rightly and well is not to add some-thing to faith; it is simply an indicator of the degree to which we have given the lordship of Jesus free rein in our lives. It is a symptom of the authenticity and purity of our faith. This is why Paul's exhortations to the Christians of his own day and to us are, at their deepest level, not appeals for greater moral exertions, but calls to recognize who we now are, as those who belong to Christ, and whose task is never other than to affirm that "belonging" with all of our heart and soul, mind and strength—in other words, whose task is never other than to believe.

6.7 THE RELATIONSHIP OF THE NEW TESTAMENT TO POLITICAL, SOCIAL, AND ECONOMIC PROBLEMS

It seems obvious that at least some and probably many questions in these areas are really *moral* questions or have strong moral components. As human beings, we are called to live out our lives not as isolated individuals, but in com-munity. We and others have real rights, and these rights touch, among other things, questions of the acquisition and distribution of money and property. Therefore if the New Testament has anything to say to the fundamental moral question ("What does it mean to act rightly and well?"), it obviously will have to address these areas of life.

But we must make one important distinction. It is true that if our judgments in political and economic matters are to be morally good, they must be made on the basis of good moral principles. However, it is important to *distinguish* political judgments from moral judgments: they are related, *but they are not the same*. In general terms, moral judgments in these areas deal with the goal or purpose of political and economic life, while political judgments deal with the question of *practical and effective means* of attaining that goal, fulfilling that purpose.

6.71 Differing Views

The question is not *whether* the New Testament has some connection with these problems, but rather *precisely what* that connection is. In attempting to give an answer, Christians take very different approaches.

Some assert that the New Testament provides us with clear moral norms to guide us in the search for economic and social justice, or at least with a way of recognizing the real values involved, of locating them precisely, and of putting them in the proper order. Others go further and insist that the New Testament imposes upon us a clear duty to give worldwide political and economic liberation top priority when we raise the question of how to act rightly and well.

All in this group argue that there are immediate conclusions, new practical imperatives, which result when unjust situations in the political, social, and economic realms are viewed in the light of the Gospel. In this sense, although they do not argue that the Gospel itself provides a blueprint for social and political action, they argue that it is an immediate source for such a blueprint. In other words, political and economic principles and programs would really be an *extension* of the Gospel, and nothing more than the adaptation of the Gospel to a new situation. For those who share this view, to proclaim the Gospel means to judge and criticize the world and its structures in the light of the Gospel.

6.72 A Better New Testament Pedigree

But there is another approach which has much stronger support in the New Testament itself. Defenders of this view argue that the New Testament gives us no *direct* and *immediate* moral guidance in these questions, and they assert that it is related to the economic and political order in very important ways, but *indirectly*. They point out that the New Testament provides the kind of liberation which makes it possible for us to approach these questions in a truly intelligent, and therefore human way. They argue that the Gospel liberates the individual Christian, freeing him to be there for the neighbor in a clever, intelligent, practical way. When they argue that the Gospel touches only the individual directly, they do *not* mean that the Gospel touches the Christian "only as an individual." There is no room in the New Testament for a "me and Jesus" piety which would restrict Christian existence to the traditional "religious" sphere (the fulfillment of moral and cultic laws). They argue that the Gospel *does* liberate the Christian for justice, and for the true concern for the political, social, and economic well-being of the neighbor, but they point out that it does this by conferring something radically new on each Christian and *not by confronting the structures of society as such*.

This approach argues that practical courses of action in the political and economic arena (whether one is pro- or anti-busing, whether one favors the ERA or not, whether one believes that the United States should stay out of

UNESCO, whether one is convinced that we should give aid directly to developing countries or only through U.N. agencies, etc.) are *not* dictated by the Gospel, but must be the fruit of expertise in political and economic matters, and must be justified and defended in these areas. In other words, for example, criticisms of both capitalism and Marxism must use good arguments from the field of economics, and not cite Gospel texts. We are all called to love the neighbor, but the question is: "How can we do that most effectively?" This approach sees the Gospel as a call to Christians to use our intelligence to promote the rights of the neighbor, and as a call which *frees* us to do just that. But this call does not tell us *how* to most effectively love the neighbor, and it does not free us from the hard work of making intelligent judgments. Such judgments must be made on the basis of facts which are usually laboriously acquired. They must be made on the basis of an honest evaluation of these facts, which often involves the task of rejecting the common nonsense which masquerades as common sense. Finally, these judgments must be made by those who are aware that, in the real world, values are often in competition and people are very imperfect, and therefore intelligent compromise is usually necessary.

As we noted in introducing it, this second approach is the one which has far better support in the New Testament. There are no political or economic norms in the New Testament, and the New Testament offers no *concrete and specific* guidance in these matters. Jesus took no position in regard to political or social or economic injustice in his day. The attempt to make Jesus into an apostle of political liberation or into an economic zealot is simply poor exegesis. He took no position, as far as we know, in respect to major economic injustices of his day, or in regard to the presence of a brutal occupying power in his country (except perhaps to say: "Give to the emperor what belongs to him and give to God what belongs to him"). He took no position in regard to the social evil of slavery which permeated the ancient world. He may have called on his followers to visit those in prison, but he did not propose a program of prison reform. He always acted as though evil was in the heart of man, and not in social, political, and economic structures as such. He never called for "structural reform." In other words, Jesus did not address political, social, and economic problems as such. For example, he said nothing about the great injustice caused by the inequitable collection of taxes. In fact, he seemed to be almost ostentatious in the way he associated with the tax collectors and welcomed them into his company. His only harsh words about oppression have to do with *religious* oppression, and were directed at those who put legal burdens on the backs of the faithful.

This emphatically does *not* mean that there is no connection between these questions and Jesus' teaching. It does *not* mean that Christians should be indifferent to injustice in any form. It does *not* mean that Christians should not be active in prison reform. But it *does* mean that there is nothing in Jesus' words or conduct which tells us *which ways* of dealing with injustice will *work* in the real world. But our task as Christians is to discover such effective ways, and not to be satisfied with solutions which are designed to make us feel "compassionate" or "caring" or "noble."

Jesus seemed to feel that money and the security it brings might distract people from the one thing necessary—total reliance on God—but he never seemed to see money in terms of social justice. He seemed to have had both the rich (at least the moderately well-to-do) and the poor among his friends, and there is no sign that he was troubled by the lack of equitable distribution of this world's goods. One indication that this really was Jesus' stance is the fact that liberation "theology" in all its forms feels the need to "improve on" Jesus, or to make excuses for him. Sometimes this is done by arguing that he shared the expectations of his contemporaries for an imminent *parousia* (second coming), and a cataclysmic end of the world, which would have obviated the need for social reform. However, these arguments are weak, and it has become clear that what Jesus offered was an essentially *religious* liberation, which implied that the human being was now free of the need to devote all his efforts to covering his tracks before God, and can devote himself to the business of living a truly *human* life.

Paul's writings offer no support for the view which would find in the New Testament a blueprint for political, social, and economic reform. In his view, the Christian message offered a basic refashioning of each human being, and not of society and its structures. (This is striking, precisely because Paul had a strong sense of the social dimension of Christian faith, and because love of neighbor was obviously, in this view, near the center of the Christian message.) Paul did not authorize revolt, but rather urged Christians to be obedient to those in authority, to work for a living, and to accommodate themselves to the political and social structures of the day, so that they would not give scandal.

6.73 An Important Caution

However, it is just as important to make the following point: if Jesus' message and Paul's theology are taken seriously, they have extremely important consequences for the political, social, and economic life of all of us. Jesus repeatedly defined love of God in terms of love of the neighbor, and Matthew's twenty fifth chapter is representative of a theme which is widely present in the Gospels and which must go back to the historical Jesus. (Note, though, that to define love of God in terms of love of the neighbor is not to identify them.) In addition, Jesus did not seem to have much use for the specifically sacral side of religion (cf. the first, second, and seventh chapters of Mark's Gospel on the questions of fasting, defilement by association with sinners, and ceremonial ablutions and dietary laws.) There is no doubt that Jesus' message has an effect on our conduct in political, social, and economic matters, *but it is all-important to specify precisely the way in which it has this effect, the way in which it works.*

6.74 Summarizing the Evidence on the Relationship of the New Testament to Questions of Political and Economic Morality

The role of the New Testament in these questions could be summed up this way. It is very real, but indirect; it does not provide norms, nor does it impose specific values. Above all, it does not propose practical solutions. For example, the New Testament makes it perfectly clear that to turn away from those on the margins of society is to turn away from Jesus, but it does not deal with this very important question: "In the real world, what policies will do the most good, realistically, for the poor, the needy, and the powerless?" And this is too important a question for us to allow it to be answered in an oversimplified way. The New Testament is certainly a call to make morally good decisions in, among other areas, political, social, and economic matters. But we act morally when we use our intelligence to discover apt and effective means to attain morally desirable goals; however, the moral desirability of our goals does not provide automatic cover for our decisions about the means to be used, and these decisions are not necessarily Christian, simply because the goals are.

The New Testament is not a political program or an economic policy statement. The New Testament does not offer political, social, or economic liberation as such. It offers religious liberation. Jesus freed people from having to rely on religious ritual and religious law to win the favor of God. Jesus freed people because he revealed the real God whom we cannot manipulate with all our religious busyness. When we receive this freedom, we are free to be our genuine selves, and to be there for the other, the neighbor.

6.8 SUMMARIZING THE ETHICAL MESSAGE OF THE NEW TESTAMENT

According to both Jesus and Paul, faith functions by healing the divided self. The New Testament is the offer of faith and the empowering of faith. The New Testament calls for faith and makes faith possible, because it is the story of a very great gift which is given (and which is offered precisely in the telling and the hearing of this story), and because it is the story of the transforming effects of that gift on human life.

There is no doubt that Jesus, as the New Testament tells his story, makes demands on us and claims us. But these demands and claims *are not law.* The Jesus-tradition of the New Testament does not tell us about the great gift which has been given so that it may put us in debt to the giver and then suggest that we can redeem this debt by acting in accordance with his will. If it did this, it would be law, and, like all law, it would awaken our resentment. (However, it must be admitted that the New Testament does not speak with one voice here. The Jesus whom we meet in

Mark's Gospel is very evidently the same as Paul's "Christ who is the end of the law," but this is not the only Jesus Christ whom we encounter in the pages of the New Testament. The Jewish-Christian community, in which and for which Matthew wrote, undoubtedly thought of Jesus as the second Moses and as the teacher of the new law, in the sense of the new way of righteousness. We meet a similar view in the letter of James, and, apart from those New Testament writings which explicitly defend it, a careful reading of Acts 15 and of Galatians 1 and 2 shows that Paul knew how widespread this other view of relationship of Christ to the law was. Otherwise, his at times bitter struggle on behalf of the law-free Gospel would not have been necessary. On matters which are close to the very heart of the Christian message, we can never avoid the question of the "canon within the canon"—that is, the question of which New Testament writings are more central to faith and for that reason make a qualitatively stronger claim on our allegiance. On some of the most essential questions, there is objective disagreement among New Testament authors, and a choice has to be made.)

The New Testament claims us because it is the story of God's gift of himself to us in Jesus Christ. Unlike other gifts, the gift of self forces us to ask an intriguing question. It forces us to ask what we are saying about ourselves if we accept this gift, and what we are saying about the kind of persons we want to be. When God gives himself in Jesus Christ, he asks if we are willing to accept the joy and the wholeness which his offer will bring. The implication, of course, is that we were un-whole, not self-sufficient, and that we needed this gift desperately. The question which we have to ask when God gives himself completely in Jesus Christ is of very great importance for our ethical activity, but it is not true that our conduct will be the *result* of new obligations which we have accepted. Rather, our conduct, our good decisions, are simply a part, an aspect, of accepting the gift. Faith is the acceptance of the totally new kind of person I have become as a result of his love. To the degree that we are, in this sense, new persons and are consciously aware of it, certain kinds of conduct (often called "good works") become simply inevitable (we could not act in any other way) and other kinds of conduct (destructive, sinful actions) become inconceivable (we simply could not do them). This is the case, not because of a law imposed from the outside, but rather because certain kinds of activity are a radical impossibility for the selves that we now are. The New Testament is not just the story of a gift before it is the story of a demand; rather, the New Testament is the story of a gift, and the *only demand is to accept the gift, totally and unrestrictedly.*

7

Conscience

7.1 INTRODUCTION

Although the word "conscience" has not been used very much up to this point, many of the problems connected both with conscience itself and with our conscience judgments have been treated under other headings. For this reason, the discussion of conscience here will provide a good summary of the thought of the entire book.

7.11 The Meaning of the Word "Conscience"

In the popular mind, conscience is that "still small voice within" which tells us whether we have done right or wrong, or, perhaps more importantly, tells us whether the decision we are considering is a good one or a bad one. According to this definition, conscience is the place within us where we feel a sense of joy and contentment when we act rightly and a sense of disquiet and guilt if we act wrongly. Popular definitions like this one can be useful at times, as starting points, but they are not very accurate, and they do not adequately distinguish conscience from other factors with which it can easily be confused. If we are going to think intelligently about conscience, we will have to subject this popular definition to some criticism.

It is very important, for example, to distinguish conscience from the compulsion to respect taboos. Taboos are the residue of pre-personal stages of religion, where powerful spiritual forces can be antagonized, not by our free decisions, but rather by our unknowing and unintentional contact with objects which are sacred to the "god" or the "demon." Primitive people experience great inner turmoil and even guilt because of the violation of these taboos, but respect for taboo is not conscience, and to act on the basis of taboos is not worthy of a human person.

It is also important to distinguish conscience from respect for mere conventions. Conventions are the usual, traditional, and accepted ways of acting within a given society. It can be useful to ask how certain conventions came into existence, because some of them may actually point to ways of acting which are worthy of being chosen. But if this is the case, they are worthy of being chosen, not because of the convention itself, but because the convention in question is a valuable way of acting and promotes real values. Conventions *as such* do not merit our loyalty, and to act in a merely conventional way or out of respect for convention is not a genuinely human way of acting.

The fact that conscience is a factor of *personal* life shows that it should also be distinguished from what is called in Freudian psychoanalytic theory the *super-ego*. The super-ego is a pre-personal principle of censorship and control, which is rooted in the desire for approval, and is therefore authority-oriented. This means simply that the super-ego is that factor of conscious life which impels people to act in such a way as to win the approval of whoever at that moment possesses authority in their lives.

7.12 A Good Definition of Conscience

Because it is easy to confuse conscience with fear of taboos or with respect for mere convention or with the superego, we must use considerable care in defining the word "conscience." One possibility would be to accept the definition which has been common in ethics and moral theology, and to refer to it as the "internal, proximate, subjective norm of morality." But, aside from the fact that these words are almost incomprehensible to the majority of intelligent people today, this definition implies that conscience is correlated with external, remote and *objective* norms of morality. And, as we have already seen, moral norms are not, in the proper sense, objective, and it is inaccurate to define the task of conscience as that of recognizing these (non-existent!) objective norms.

When moral theologians developed the definition of conscience, given in the preceding paragraph, what they meant (in modern terms) was probably this: conscience is a judgment about a way of acting which I am now considering. It is the judgment that this way of acting is either worthy or unworthy of being chosen, and that therefore I *should* or *should not* choose it. Here we will use the term "conscience judgment" to refer to this, and we will use the simple term "conscience" to refer to the habitual ability to make such judgments, or to the way in which such judgments are ordinarily made. This ability consists in the presence of a number of other, deeper judgments which have been made and renewed over a period of time.

Among these deeper judgments which are constitutive of conscience are the general normative judgments which we fashion for ourselves in the different areas of life (for example, the spheres of social and economic justice, honesty and integrity, the use of our sexuality, professional responsibility). Underlying these are the judgments which we make about the essential values of life—self-love, love of neighbor, responsibility for the rest of creation. And, of course, underlying all of these is the foundational judgment that values *are* objective, that there are ways of acting which in and of themselves are worthy of being chosen, and that these values call on us to be responsible for them and responsive to them. This is the deepest judgment of all, and it is the one which really expresses, at the deepest level, the kind of person I want to be. These deeper judgments are included in every conscience judgment, as its presupposition, its basis, and its support. For clarity, it is better not to confuse them with conscience, but to see them as the basis and ground of good conscience judgments and of the good conscience.

7.13 Some Important Distinctions

In talking about the conscience *judgment,* and about conscience (in the strict sense) as the *power to make such judgments,* it is useful to make several distinctions. First of all, we can distinguish a *correct* conscience from an *incorrect* conscience. A correct conscience judgment is one which is objectively true because it conforms to objective values and to relationships which exist outside the one making the judgment. An incorrect conscience judgment is a mistaken or erroneous judgment and it results from the failure to perceive values which are really there, and/or from the failure to perceive their proper order and relationship among themselves.

There is another very important distinction which should not be confused with the preceding one. A *good* conscience, or a *good* conscience judgment, results from the serious attempt to locate the values in life and to respect their proper relationship and order, using all reasonable means to do so. A *bad* conscience, or conscience judgment, results from the willingness to ignore value, to let pseudo-values masquerade as real ones, and to resign from the task of seeking value.

A conscience judgment (and conscience itself as the ability to make such judgments habitually) can be *good* but *incorrect* (and this is not at all uncommon), because the "goodness" of conscience comes not from its objective correctness, but rather from the *serious effort* to make it correctly. In addition to this, at least some of the general normative judgments which are the basis of conscience can be good but incorrect (if we have done what is in our power to make them correctly, but have, as a matter of fact, not succeeded). However, the foundational or transcendental judgment about value (that values really exist, independent of our likes and dislikes) *cannot be good but incorrect,* because the call to accept the objectivity of value is so central to our humanity that we cannot reject this call without knowing it and being guilty of acting in such a way. *It is this fact which marks the place where relativism ends in moral matters.* (Incidentally, it is possible for a conscience judgment to be "bad" but "correct." Such a judgment is one which is made carelessly and irresponsibly and with the suspicion that it may lead to some harmful and destructive results, but which, by accident, happens to be correct.)

7.14 Conscience and the Moral Act

It might seem from what has been said so far that the conscience judgment tells us how we are to act, and that this judgment is then followed by our decision to act or not to act in that way—followed, that is, by an act of will in which we determine to follow or to reject the advice of conscience.

This would locate the moral act in the decision to follow or reject such advice, but this is not really the way the process of decision-making works. It is much more accurate to locate the moral act *in the conscience judgment itself*. We do wrong, not by rejecting the clear demands of our conscience judgments, but by *tampering* with them. We do wrong by forcing the conscience judgment to say what some fragmented part of us *wants* it to say. We do wrong by substituting the super-ego, or some distorted set of value judgments for a valid conscience judgment and then insisting that this distorted judgment is really the one to be followed. We do wrong by deliberately remaining in the dark about matters of fact or matters of principle, and by giving pseudo-values the appearance of real ones.

This holds true also for those deeper judgments which underlie the conscience judgment and which are its ground and basis. Here, too, we act rightly insofar as we make good judgments; we act wrongly in "allowing" ourselves to make bad judgments, by not examining the facts and by not facing reality. In fact, it is here that we are most responsible, because it is here that we either allow ourselves to be claimed by reality or that we reject its claim. It is here that we decide either to serve God or to play God. *To put it simply: the fashioning and forming of the good conscience judgment is the good moral act.*

7.2 THE OBLIGATIONS IMPOSED BY CONSCIENCE

7.21 Do We Have an Obligation To Follow Our Consciences?

Conscience judgments always make use of the word "should": that is, they are always statements that, in a con-

crete situation, we *should* act in one way rather than another. This raises an interesting question: Is there an
absolute obligation to follow one's own conscience? The
right and duty of following one's own conscience has become almost the central (if not the only!) moral principle
of non-theistic humanism since the Enlightenment, and it
is a favorite slogan of people who talk about ethics from a
merely humanist perspective. ("Non-theistic" humanism is
a term more commonly used by groups in Europe to describe themselves. Their view is that God may or may not
exist, but that whether he does or not, he is not relevant to
human concerns. I use the term "humanism" with some
misgiving, because of its rather sloppy use by the religious
right to characterize *any* view which is not fundamentalistic
and anti-intellectual.) Many in this country who would
characterize themselves as "humanists" speak of the serious
obligation one has to follow his/her own conscience, and of
the obligation which we have to respect the rights of all people to follow their consciences, as long as others are not
harmed by their actions. We have already pointed out in
earlier sections of this book that statements of this type represent a serious confusion of two quite distinct questions:
the first is the question of the moral responsibility of the
individual to make good moral judgments and the second
is the question of the purpose and competence of the law.

7.22 The Moral Responsibility of the Individual

Instead of speaking of the obligation of *following* conscience, we do better to point out that such an obligation
can exist only if the conscience and the conscience judgment are *good*—that is, only if we have used all reasonable
means to discover the real values in life, and to find those
ways of acting which in and of themselves are worthy of

being chosen. Our real obligation is to *fashion* or to *form* our consciences in the right way, and this means simply that we are obliged to commit ourselves willingly and deliberately to the truth. It means that we are called on to be *attentive*, open to the truth. It means that we are called on to be *deliberately intelligent,* to understand the facts and principles involved. It means that we are called on to be *reasonable,* to make serious efforts to draw correct conclusions from the judgments which we make. And it means that we are called on to be *responsible*—that is, to willingly act in the real world in accordance with the truth which we have found.

To form one's conscience well is to be deliberately discerning, that is, to strive to distinguish real values from pseudo-values and to distinguish common sense from common nonsense. To form one's conscience is to develop clever plans for protecting and promoting value and to foresee difficulties which may arise and to devise ways of circumventing them. To form one's conscience is to be willing to learn from others, to observe the way in which intelligent people act now, and have acted in the past. To form one's conscience is to deliberately do what is in our power to remove ignorance of facts and of principles. In summary, to form one's conscience is to be critical, to examine the judgments which we have made, to ask whether they have been made on the basis of evidence or on the basis of slogans.

This brief discussion of the obligation of forming one's conscience will make it possible to raise the question of sin in a new way. Sin can now be defined as the *deliberate failure to form one's conscience as one should.* It would even be possible to take the classical terms of the tradition—mortal (or serious) sin, and venial (not so serious) sin—and to define them in terms of the new approach suggested here. Mortal sin would be deliberate failure in those deep and essential judgments about the values of life—those judgments which underlie and support our individual conscience judgments. The assumption, of course, is that the failure in those deep judgments is not the failure to have a *correct* conscience, but the failure to have a *good* conscience—a failure for which one is responsible, because in the deepest sense one *intends* it. Such a failure can only come from the deliberate attempt to play God. This failure in the underlying judgment is *revealed* in the conscience judgment about some particular matter or issue, but obviously the term "sin" should not be used to refer to the external action; it refers rather to the intention, to the judgment of intent which precedes it. The term "sin" should be used to refer to the bad conscience judgment which springs from the willingness to remain in the dark about the demands which reality makes upon us. If these demands are the most basic and fundamental demands of life, then the willingness to remain in the dark about them and to pretend that they really do not claim us is properly called "serious (or mortal) sin." In this framework, venial sin would be a bad conscience judgment which does not engage the deepest level of the person and therefore does not touch the level at which the underlying value judgments in the different areas of life are made.

7.3 CONSCIENCE, NORMS, AND THE LAW OF GOD

7.31 The Traditional Approach

Traditionally, as we have seen, the conscience judgment was understood as the application of objective norms to a specific case, that is, it was understood as the act of internalizing and accepting objective moral norms, insofar as they were applicable to the case at hand. However, in this book we have spoken, not of objective norms, but of objective *values,* and in line with this, we will speak of the conscience judgment as one which identifies the value[s] in a concrete situation, and draws concrete conclusions about appropriate ways of acting.

It has been common to say that conscience is good, in so far as it accepts the law of God, or even that the good conscience is constituted as such by the acceptance of the law of God, and it is possible to find phrases to this effect even in the documents of the Second Vatican Council. In using the term "law of God," the Council was apparently referring to the will of God, and in terms of the scholastic philosophy and theology of law, this use of the term makes sense. However, in a non-scholastic age like the one we live in, "law" is not a good term to use. It emphasizes the will of the lawmaker at the expense of the intelligence of those subject to the law, and it almost always connotes the imposition of a sanction. For precisely this reason, it misses the essential relation between conscience and intelligence.

7.32 CONSCIENCE AND FREEDOM

It is extremely important to see the conscience judgment as the exercise of freedom. The word "freedom" here must, or course, be understood in the proper sense; it does not refer to indifference, or to the power to make arbitrary and unmotivated choices. Freedom is the power to create the real self—the self which God calls us to be. Forming conscience in the right way is an essential, and, in fact, *the* essential exercise of freedom, and this brings up a specifically Catholic problem which is connected with the formation of conscience.

7.4 THE TEACHING AUTHORITY OF THE CHURCH AND THE CONSCIENCE OF THE CATHOLIC

7.41 The Nature of the Problem

In all religious organizations, the clergy (or whatever those in the management sector are called) claim the right and duty to teach. However, it seems safe to say that it is particularly in the Catholic Church that this right and duty is exercised with greater regularity and assurance than in any other religious body. Popes, councils (meetings of bishops from all parts of the world), as well as individual bishops, claim the right to instruct Catholics in matters of faith and of moral or ethical activity; rather than claiming simply the right to teach or to instruct, they claim the right to tell members of the Church how they are to act and not to act in these areas.

If churchmen claimed only to be of assistance in identifying values and in putting them in their proper relationship, there would certainly be no problem. But churchmen claim to teach *authoritatively* and they demand obedience to that authority; it is this claim which causes the problems, and many people feel that it is this claim which conflicts with the freedom which conscience itself demands. For if the conscience judgment is a deeply personal act and therefore the exercise of freedom, then it would seem impossible to understand it as the act of obedience to a command— here, the command of an authoritative teaching body within the Church.

This problem points to a certain ambiguity in the word "authority." Etymologically, the word is derived from a Latin root which means "increase" and the noun originally meant "the quality of being an originator, the source of some positive and productive way of acting." But in the course of time, the word "authority" has come to mean "that quality in virtue of which one must be obeyed." In view of this ambiguity, we might ask this question: "When church-men claim the right to teach authoritatively, do they only claim the right to train the members of the Church to make good conscience judgments, or do they intend to lay down the law?" In point of fact, it seems clear that, with very few exceptions, they have intended to lay down the law.

7.42 The Sources of Authority in the Church

Authority in the Church is rooted in the fact that the Gospel, the good news, is not merely theoretical truth; it is truth which has many consequences for decision-making and for the practical business of human living. Further-more, instruction of the members of the Church is a basic function of Church life. The earliest writings in the New Testament which deal with the question of instruction are those of Paul, and therefore it is appropriate that we turn to him first.

Paul seemed to feel that instruction of the members of the Church was a task shared by all members of the com-munity, but there is no doubt that he himself exercised this function with great self-assurance, and that he felt justified in doing this on the grounds that he was an apostle. It is also clear that Paul felt that his rights and responsibilities touched not only matters of doctrine, but matters of moral and ethical activity as well. Further, he seemed to feel that there were some people in each community who were called upon to exercise this right and to undertake this obligation of instruction in a special way. The group in Philippi whom he called "teachers" seem to have fulfilled this function, al-though we should note that in Paul's own time the existence of priests and bishops as distinct groups with clearly defined rights and competences is extremely doubtful.

For Paul, this task and obligation of teaching authoritatively is simply part of the task of building up the Church. Paul's own experience with disorder and confusion in the Church in Corinth probably led him to appreciate the importance of authority more and more in the course of his ministry. Paul probably died in the early sixties, and in the churches which he had founded, as well as some others, those who followed him attempted to give Church life continuity and stability. Toward the end of the first century and at the beginning of the second, the task of instruction in matters of faith and morals began to be taken over by members of a group called *episkopoi*—those who were "overseers" or "superintendents" of the community. Although at the beginning of this period there seem to have been a number of these *episkopoi* in each local church, all of whom shared responsibility, as time went on the rule came to be that there would be one *episkopos* per local community—a fact often referred to as the development of the "monarchical episcopacy." It is very possible that this system developed because the earlier, collegial exercise of authority had led to disputes and strife.

7.43 The Historical Development of Authoritative Teaching after New Testament Times

In the second and third centuries, these *episkopoi* (and from then on we can properly call them "bishops") began more and more to exercise a teaching role within their own churches. From about the middle of the third century on, these bishops often acted not simply as individuals, but they began to act in concert: that is, they met at *synods* and decided both doctrinal and ethical questions. The first *general* synod or *council* took place in the year 325 A.D., and it was a meeting of all the bishops of the Church, at least in theory and in principle. In the period from 325 to 451, three more of these general or *ecumenical* councils hammered out the doctrines on God, Christ, the Spirit, and the Trinity, which still form the basis of our credal statements today.

During this entire period (more properly: from about the mid-point of the third century), the Bishop of Rome claimed a unique kind of authority, and exercised, as his own prerogative, the function of teacher of the universal Church. In addition to Italy itself, his claim seems to have been accepted, sometimes grudgingly, by the churches of the East, by the powerful church of North Africa, as well as by the numerically less significant churches of Gaul and Spain. There seems to have been some uncertainty as to whether the Bishop of Rome exercised this role because he was the successor of Peter, or rather because Rome was the imperial capital. The Roman Bishops themselves insisted that it was the first reason which counted, while the patriarchs of the Eastern Churches were increasingly inclined toward the second. This was to become a serious problem when, early in the fourth century, Constantine transferred the imperial capital from Rome to the new city on the shores of the Bosporos, which bore his name. During and after the Germanic invasions in the West, the Bishops of Rome continued their practice of teaching authoritatively, and in the Western sections of the old empire their authority was generally accepted. But, increasingly, Constantinople and those parts of the East which were dependent on it drifted away from Rome and were not inclined to recognize a special teaching office of the Bishop of Rome.

Under Gregory VII, who was Pope toward the end of

the eleventh century, and under Innocent III, who was Pope at the beginning of the thirteenth century, papal authority reached a peak which has probably never been surpassed. Their authority extended not only to religious questions but to civil matters as well, and these Popes claimed the right to depose kings and emperors. The Protestant Reformation of the early sixteenth century was, among other things, a rejection of these very broad papal claims, and in reacting to the Reformation the Catholic Church at the Council of Trent (1545 to 1564) tried to restore the medieval status quo with a strong reassertion of papal power. In the years since the Counterreformation, the secular, temporal power of the papacy declined virtually to the vanishing point, but during the same period, papal power within the Church grew. Under Pius XII, who died in 1958, there was an enormous quantitative increase in papal teaching, and in a constant stream of addresses which touched on almost every aspect of modern life, this austere but widely venerated Pope asserted, more forcefully than any Pope in modern times, the papal claim to teach with authority and to be entitled to obedience by all in the church.

The pontificate of Pius XII was the culmination of about a century of development, during which a quite distinctive style of papal teaching emerged. This style strongly emphasized papal *authority,* and it saw papal teaching, not merely as providing information which would help in the formation of conscience, but rather as constituting an imperative which could not be rejected in good faith. In other words, the acceptance of papal teaching was regarded as essential to the formation of a good conscience. During the same period, papal teaching was not sympathetic to the notion that human beings undergo fundamental changes in history, and that changed circumstances may, at times, imply a change in moral imperatives. This theology was most comfortable with scholastic thought and with its notion of human nature as stable and unchanging. Many moral theologians today feel that, even when infallibility was not formally invoked, papal teaching was regarded as irreformable, precisely because it rested either on the unchanging law of God or on immutable human nature which was not subject to the vagaries of the historical process. Finally, from our perspective today, it seems clear that much papal teaching during the period in question did not view the modern world and its concerns with sympathy or with hope, and did not see this world as a challenge, but rather as a threat.

In some respects, the Second Vatican Council represented a break with this style of papal teaching, and it was at this Council that the majority of the bishops (with the enthusiastic support of the new Pope, John XXIII) made the first tentative moves toward developing a concept of authority which would be more *biblical* in inspiration, and at the same time more suited to a Church trying to live in the real world of the late twentieth century. Although Vatican II reasserted the doctrine of Vatican I on the primacy and infallibility of the Pope, the net effect of both the content and the style of its teaching has been to make the exercise of papal authority more pastoral and more collegial, and to make papal teaching itself more sympathetic to the concerns and hopes of the modern world and less dependent on the "Church as a bulwark" model of the pre-conciliar period.

7.44 Our Situation Today

It seems clear, to judge from this brief historical survey, that until the very recent past, the general tendency in the Catholic Church has been toward increasing the authority of the hierarchy and especially that of the Pope. When confronted with the teaching of the hierarchy, the task of the laity was simply to obey. As papal authority grew, it was not clear what functions theologians were to fulfill in the process of discovering and teaching the truth, and many members of the hierarchy probably regarded them as what we would call today "resource persons," who might be consulted when papal or episcopal teaching was being formulated.

Developments at Vatican II led to the question of whether the whole Church—the hierarchy, the theological community, and the laity—may be at once a teaching Church and a learning Church. More than anything else, it was the development of new and better ways of reading Scripture, particularly the New Testament, which led to questions of this type, although a better knowledge of history and of the various factors which condition human understanding all played a role as well.

Today as a result of these insights we are in a position to raise, in a new and perhaps better way, the question of the relationship of the teaching authority of the Church to the conscience judgment of the individual Catholic, and we can begin to formulate an answer which respects several factors: the Gospel itself and its statements about authority, the historical facts about the development of authority in the Church, and the signs of our own times—that is, the unique challenge of the closing years of the twentieth century. Among these signs of the times are the values which we have learned to esteem in the exercise of civil liberty and personal responsibility. Furthermore, today we recognize, more than at any other time in the history of the Church, that the task of preserving, expressing, and deepening the faith is incumbent on all—on the hierarchy, on the theological community, and on the laity. With this in mind, we can propose, in outline form, an answer to the question of how the teaching authority of the Church is related to the conscience judgment of the individual Christian. This outline is based on observation of what seems to be happening in the Church today, and on reflections on that process by moral and systematic theologians.

7.45 Facts Which Are Important for a Solution

We should begin by mentioning some facts which are widely accepted by scholars in a number of branches of theology. *First:* good exegesis is making it increasingly clear that in the earliest Pauline churches, authority was essentially charismatic—it was not exercised in virtue of an office which one possessed, but rather in virtue of one's having been given the gift of the Spirit—that is, the personal power of God which moves wherever it wants and settles on those whom it chooses. In this sense, Paul's own authority was charismatic. As he states in Galatians, he was not chosen by the other apostles, nor was he instructed by them. Rather, he traces his apostolate back to an encounter with the risen Lord. In this connection, we should note that there is a strong consensus on the part of competent exegetes that those Gospel texts which support the hierarchical principle (the exercise of authority in virtue of office) are most probably not words of the historical Jesus, but constructions of the Christian communities of the second and third generations.

The *second* fact is equally important: there were problems with this charismatic authority; disorder and even rebellion were rampant in the Pauline churches, and charismatic authority, even when exercised by Paul, provided no effective way of dealing with these problems which were serious enough to threaten the very existence of the Church. As a result of these difficulties, the hierarchical principle developed in New Testament times, and the New Testament itself legitimates this development. In fact, a critical reading of the New Testament suggests that if authority is to be exercised in the proper way, both the hierarchical and the charismatic elements are needed.

The *third* fact to keep in mind is that, in the view of many Catholic Scripture scholars, the development of the hierarchical principle in the Catholic Church during the high Middle Ages, and again in the post-Tridentine era, is not fully legitimated by the New Testament. It is not precisely infallibility or jurisdictional primacy which these scholars see as lacking a good New Testament pedigree, but rather the extension of papal authority to areas well outside questions of faith and moral life, and, during the post-Tridentine period, the centralization of power in the Roman Curia to a degree which at times made the bishops look like proconsuls or administrators of curial policy. Probably the fact that, after Constantine, union of church and state was the rule and not the exception was responsible for the absence of the spirit of collegiality in Church government; as long as the empire provided the model, it is not surprising that the hierarchical Church reflected, in its power structure, the various forms of governance which were in fashion from the time of Rome to the age of revolution. However, although the hierarchical principle and the Petrine office are both firmly grounded in the New Testament, other trappings of absolutism are no more normative for the government of the Church than they are for civil society.

The *fourth* fact to keep in mind is that this absolutist model has been increasingly questioned during the past century and a half. This was particularly true in Europe after the Second World War, and Vatican II was one very important symptom of growing alienation of many European lay Catholics and theologians from a papacy which defined itself in very authoritarian terms. Widespread discontent with the autocratic style of Pius XII was a major factor in the success of the reforming wins at the Second Vatican Council.

The *fifth* fact to keep in mind is that developments in Scripture studies and a less defensive reading of Church history led a number of Catholic theologians, in the period after the Second World War, to question the authoritarian model of papal teaching; and this, in turn, led to strong defensive reactions on the part of the hierarchy, and especially on the part of the Pope and the papal administrative apparatus in Rome. This reaction led, particularly during and after the Second Vatican Council, to polarization instead of dialogue between the hierarchy and the theological community.

Members of the hierarchy have seen their role as that of preserving doctrinal purity and conserving the substance of the ancient faith, and for this reason they have tended to favor theologians with traditionalist leanings. On the other hand, theologians have seen their role as that of making traditional doctrine more understandable and more serviceable for the changing needs of the Church, and they have tended to be more open to new ways of expressing old truths. These tendencies on the part of the hierarchy and the theologians have led, especially during the past twenty-five years, to a number of unfortunate confrontations. Theologians have seen their task as that of pulling what they see as a largely recalcitrant hierarchy into the modern world, while members of the hierarchy have seen their task as that of holding in check radical theologians who seek change for its own sake and who have little or no respect for the doctrinal and moral tradition of the Church. This adversarial relationship is certainly not a healthy one.

The *sixth* fact to keep in mind is that, regardless of whether one approves of this or not, the majority of Catholics in Western Europe and North America will accept Church teaching as a very important *factor* which must be acknowledged in forming one's conscience; but they will not accept Church teaching as something from which it is impossible to disagree in good faith. The old adage *Roma locuta, causa finita* (Rome has spoken and that is the end of the matter) is no longer generally accepted, and it is important to note that this fact is widely acknowledged, both by those who approve of this stance and by those who strongly disapprove.

7.46 The Role of Consensus in the Teaching of the Church

Many Catholic theologians today are of the opinion that instruction and teaching on moral questions will be most effective when the hierarchy, the theological community, and the laity cooperate in fashioning a consensus— a consensus which is based on a common understanding of the factors involved in making the Christian conscience judgment. This common understanding itself should be based on Scripture, and due note should be taken of the way in which Scripture has been understood and misunderstood throughout the ages. When this consensus is reached, it is appropriate for it to be articulated for the benefit of all by those who hold pastoral office in the Church—the Pope and the bishops. The development of this consensus will not come about by balancing the independent claims of any of the groups involved; it will only come about when we recognize the different but complementary functions of hierarchy, theologians, and laity. A conservative hierarchy, pulling against a radical theological community, leaving a confused laity in the middle, does not represent a responsible division of powers and competences.

7.47 The Responsibilities of All in the Church

The three groups mentioned here should recognize that they have not only rights but also real obligations to each other and to the Church; and they should recognize that they will fulfill these obligations more effectively by trying to understand each other's viewpoints than they will by staking out adversarial positions. Members of the hierarchy do not possess an *automatic* charism which guarantees the acquisition of truth without study and without consultation with others, and they will probably serve the Church most effectively, not by trying to impose teaching from on high, but rather by trying to articulate a consensus which has come into being through intelligent dialogue and through careful observation of Christian practice. The wording of the recent pastoral letters of the bishops of the United States seems to indicate their conviction that they will be more effective as teachers if they offer guidelines instead of giving orders.

Members of the hierarchy have a special responsibility in matters of dogma (questions of the official teaching of the Church which is binding on all), but even here their task is not simply to preserve what is of value in the past, but also to develop the teaching of the Church. Part of their task is to see that this teaching does not simply remain *verbally* the same, but actually continues to proclaim the same message in new and different words which are required because, with the passage of time, human beings develop new and different ways of thinking and of expressing their thoughts. The hierarchy will fulfill this part of their task by remaining in dialogue with the theological community, and by creating a climate in which theological research can flourish and peer-group criticism among theologians is the principal means of insuring that theological research helps in the building up of the Church. It is certainly the special task and competence of the hierarchy to preserve and conserve the deposit of faith, but this does not imply that conservative theologians (in the popular sense of "conservative") have privileged access to the truth.

Theologians have some serious obligations too. They should recognize that they are responsible to the Church and not simply to themselves as individuals or as a group. They should be aware of the fact that there are some theological truths (or at least facts of which theologians are convinced) which may be pastorally counterproductive at a given moment in the life of the Church, and they should know that a theology which is not essentially pastoral (that is, not motivated by a desire to build up the Church) is quite simply not good theology.

Theologians should recognize that continuity with the past is a value, and that preserving this continuity is also part of the task of the theological community, and not simply that of the hierarchy. Authentic growth will always take place in continuity with the past, and it occurs when the Church meets a contemporary challenge through a creative application of its own inner resources, and not when a response is forced upon it by a trendy pressure group. As members of the Church, we should not be at the mercy of every new trend, every passing fad, and it should be obvious to all that theologians whose only abiding fear is that of being passed on the left are not serving the Church.

The theological community should be self-critical, not only in matters of scholarship, but precisely in respect to the task of building up the Church. This last-mentioned obligation is one which seems to be neglected today, and theologians who depart radically from ancient and constant teaching can feel quite sure that they will not be called to task, even by respected members of the theological fraternity. (The teaching referred to here touches matters of faith and of moral conduct which are dealt with in the New Testament itself.) It may be that this neglect of peer-group criticism is yet another unfortunate effect of the polarization of theological positions, and, even more, of Church life, which seems to have come about since 1980. Perhaps theologians are afraid that their criticism of other scholars will be used by Roman authorities in an updated version of the anti-Modernist campaign in the early years of this century, and it may be that their fears are not entirely unfounded. But it does seem strange that theologians, who frequently argue that, instead of censure by Rome, their work should be subject only to peer-group criticism, engage so rarely in this latter exercise.

The members of the laity have some obligations in these matters as well. They should do everything in their power to keep from severing the bond which links them to the hierarchy and to all others in the Church. They should not use clerical arrogance or incompetence as an excuse for excommunicating themselves. Those who cease participating in the liturgy and who turn away from the sacramental life of the Church may themselves be able to live out the rest of their lives on the capital and the patrimony of their Catholic past, but they are likely to have children who are Christians in name but pagans in fact. For this reason, members of the laity should be careful to distinguish between the hierarchy and the Church. Furthermore, members of the laity have the obligation to be well-informed, in proportion to their education and intelligence. And, finally, they have the duty of respecting the positive intent and the underlying purpose of the teaching of the hierarchy, even when they may, in good faith, act counter to that teaching.

7.48 The Teaching Authority of the Church and the Conscience of the Individual

When we ask what role the teaching authority of the hierarchy ought to play when the individual Catholic undertakes the task of forming his/her conscience, we find that there are three elements in the answer. First, we have to admit that it is not the role of even authoritative teaching to replace the conscience judgment of the individual Catholic. The authority of the hierarchy is not precisely that of making conscience judgments for the laity and then simply demanding that these judgments be accepted as correct. Second, members of the laity, and theologians, ought to weigh the teaching of Popes and bishops very carefully, and if they act contrary to these guidelines, they should do so only for serious reasons and when, after intelligent discussion with others, they have come to the conclusion that this is the only course of action which is open to them. Third, those who do act in a way contrary to the guidelines of the hierarchy should remain self-critical, and they should ask themselves if there are motives other than the search for truth which may have led them to act as they do. Fourth, those who teach views which diverge from those of the hierarchy should make this fact very clear to their readers and their listeners. When there is a strong consensus of the hierarchy on some point, those who dissent from such a consensus should not present their views as those of "the

Church" or as solutions to questions on which there is no official teaching. Dissent is necessary and it can be responsible, but it must be honest. Even non-infallible teaching makes a legitimate claim on our loyalty as Catholics.

7.5 THE CHRISTIAN CONSCIENCE JUDGMENT: A SUMMARY

7.51 The Basis of the Christian Conscience Judgment

The conscience judgment which one makes specifically as a Christian is a response to a *new situation*—that situation which is outlined in the New Testament, and which is realized (= made real) when that book is read, heard, preached, discussed, and acted upon in the Christian community. With the coming of Jesus and with the response to that coming, which is the New Testament—a response which continues and prolongs his coming—God has created a new world. In this new world, the defining conditions of human existence have been changed. Since the coming of Jesus Christ, human beings live on a new earth under a new heaven. We ourselves are different, and we stand in the presence of a new and heretofore unknown God. In this new world, a radically different kind of conscience judgment has become possible.

The new situation which became objectively real with the coming of Jesus, and which becomes real for each individual as he/she comes to faith, replaces an old situation. This old situation is one in which we were in the grip of various compulsions, all of them rooted in the basic drive to make our own lives secure by asserting ourselves against the world and against the neighbor. Left to ourselves, we accept these compulsions and the pseudo-values to which they give rise. We do this because we resent our dependence on God, and in a perverse way we have the power to create a world of our own which is independent of God. In this world which is the work of our own hands, intelligence becomes a means of holding this world of our own together by manipulating others and by weakening them in order to achieve a position of relative strength and security. Intelligence becomes a way of controlling one's entire environment. This misuse of intelligence is the essence of sin, for it is the refusal of truth.

In and of ourselves, we are implicated in this situation, "caught" in it, and we can do nothing to extricate ourselves. We need to be liberated from these pseudo-values and compulsions; we need to be liberated from our refusal of the truth about God, about the world, about our neighbor, and about ourselves. The Christian message about the God who accepts us unconditionally brings precisely this liberation. It solves the problem of our insecurity, because God's acceptance of us is a pure gift which we can do nothing to merit. Because God gives security, there are no "terminal" threats—no threats which have the power to destroy our existence once and for all. God's unconditional acceptance frees us from our pseudo-values and it frees us from misusing intelligence manipulatively to pay homage to them. God's acceptance frees us to use our intelligence as he intended: to discover ways to be there effectively for the neighbor, to discover ways to love the neighbor.

The Christian message does this in and through the event called "faith"—not because faith is the acceptance of principles which would then determine our conduct, but because faith is the act of allowing God to claim us, accept us as his own, without conditions and without any bound or limit. Because faith is the act of accepting God in this way, it is also the act of accepting ourselves, as the ones claimed in this way by God, and for this reason faith brings integration and wholeness. It makes freedom possible, because it offers a vision of a real self worth affirming. Faith is the act in which we accept God, and in which we accept his acceptance of us. Because faith is our acceptance of God, who is the ground and basis of objective value, faith includes the foundational judgment which is the basis and form of every good conscience judgment, as well as the foundation of morally good existence: the judgment that there are absolute values which are not of our own making, but which claim us unconditionally.

Faith is the response to the real God, and it makes a truly human existence possible. We are human only when we stand in the presence of this God, and are, in virtue of this fact, free to use our intelligence on behalf of real people—that is, all who have been called into being by this God. Genuine faith makes the good conscience judgment possible. The good conscience judgment and the good moral act (they are really the same) are actions which are intelligent and free. As is always the case, faith adds nothing to human intelligence and freedom, nor does it conflict with them or compete with them for our loyalty. Rather, it empowers them, makes them possible. This is the final word on the relation of faith to the morally good decision.

7.52 The Good Conscience Judgment in Itself

In making a good conscience judgment we examine a projected way of acting, a specific action which it is possible for us to perform or omit, and we make an assessment or a judgment about the values which will become concrete or the values which will be destroyed if we act in such a way. In other words, we examine a projected way of acting, and judge it to be either the embodiment of an ideal or as the rejection of an ideal. As we have seen, very many projected actions will be *mixed*—concretizing some values while rejecting others. In such cases, the conscience judgment will be an over-all assessment of the values which are at stake, and will include the attempt to measure their relative importance, and therefore to evaluate the kind of claim they make on us.

Such a good conscience judgment has a number of components or elements. What we have called "the foundational judgment"—that is, our conviction that there are ways of acting which are (un)worthy of being chosen, regardless of who knows it and likes it—is the basic component of every good conscience judgment. In addition, behind every good conscience judgment there stand a number of good normative judgments or *norms* which we have fashioned. As we have seen, these norms do not exist *as such* outside us; they are rather the judgments which we make about objective values and about practical and effective ways of protecting and promoting those values.

The serious and persevering effort to construct such norms is precisely what could be called the formation of the Christian conscience, and it is this on-going commitment which shows that one is living in grace and not in sin. It is this serious and persevering effort which is constitutive of good character, and because this effort will issue in a series of individually good choices and of individual actions which promote value, it makes no sense to play a morality of character off against a morality of action. Actions are the revelation of character and they are constitutive of character, and this is above all true of those actions in which we create good moral norms.

There is a third component of the good conscience judgment, and that is the commitment to understand precisely what is at stake in an individual, projected action.

This commitment is the honest effort to see the individual, projected action as it *really* is, and not to let wishful thinking have its way. It is the honest effort to see the values which would become historically real, if we choose rightly, and the attempt to look honestly at the damage done, if we choose wrongly. It is the effort to get beneath surface appearances to the reality of the situation, and, perhaps above all, it is the effort to be self-critical, to become sensitive to the results which we "want" to emerge from the examination, and to cultivate a healthy suspicion of our ability to tinker with the facts in order to produce the desired result. In other words, the good conscience judgment emerges from what we have defined as "the good conscience," an habitual disposition, a constant willingness to get at the truth, and to act on whatever imperatives emerge when the truth is found.

7.53 The Morally Good Decision

The morally good decision *is* the good conscience judgment; it is not a subsequent decision. The old notion that the conscience judgment is the last practical judgment which precedes the actual decision to act or not act was the product of a defective psychology which compartmentalized the human mind into separate pigeon holes called "intellect" and "will," which were related only superficially and externally. The judgments which we make about how to act are not really numerable and neatly distinguishable from each other. It is particularly important to note that the free act, the exercise of human freedom, is not the *arbitrary* choice of either virtue or vice, when we are confronted with the clear conscience judgment which identifies a particular act as either one or the other. Here, as always, the free act is not the exercise of arbitrariness; it is the act in which we create the authentic self we are called to be, by deliberately striving to locate the values in life and to devise ways of protecting and promoting them. The free act is the choice of light over darkness, above all when the confusion and the uncertainty of darkness would apparently permit us to continue in courses of action to which a part of us is powerfully drawn, but which we suspect are not really worthy of us. The free act is the choice of truth over error, above all when we are tempted to cultivate and favor our erroneous judgments, because they seem to justify ways of acting with which we have grown comfortable, but which we suspect would not be able to stand the light of day.

7.54 The Christian Moral Imperative

This implies that the moral imperative for Christians is never "obey the law (of God, of Christ, of the Church)." The one and only moral imperative is "be deliberately intelligent" (in the sense which "intelligent" always has in this book: open to reality, committed to understanding it and to drawing correct conclusions from what we have understood, so that we can respond appropriately to the real needs of real people in the real world).

This kind of commitment to intelligence is possible only when insecurity and the fear which is consequent on it have been driven from the center of the human heart. In the Christian view, there is only one thing, one fact, which can bring about this peace and this security: the conviction that we are accepted, affirmed, sustained, and supported by One who will allow no obstacle to interfere; that we are loved by God with an everlasting love, and that the *only* demand which he makes on us is to let him get away with precisely that—being the unconditional lover. The Christian moral imperative is, finally, "become what you (already) are; begin to think and act like those who are loved without bound or limit, by one who will not allow even our own sinfulness to obstruct that love." It was this insight which led Augustine to frame the apparently dangerous but perfectly sound summary of all Christian morality: "Love and do what(ever) you want." We can love because God has loved us first, and our first and greatest act of love is letting him be the one he wants to be. When we have done this, then "whatever we want" is certain to be a good choice; under these conditions we could not possibly want anything else.

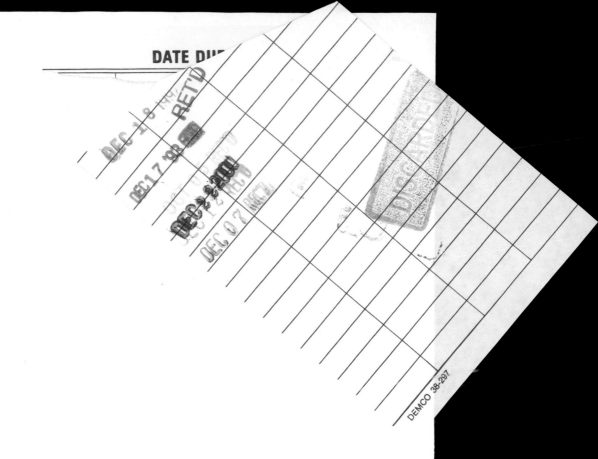